The Ailing Empire

Also by Sebastian Haffner

THE MEANING OF HITLER

The Ailing Empire

Germany from Bismarck to Hitler

by

SEBASTIAN HAFFNER

Translated by

JEAN STEINBERG

Fromm International Publishing Corporation
New York

Library of Congress Cataloging-in-Publication Data
Haffner, Sebastian.
The ailing empire.
Translation of: Von Bismarck zu Hitler.
Includes index.
1. Germany—History—1870–
2. Germany—History—1848–1870. I. Title.
DD220.H2513   1989   943.08   88-33491
ISBN 0-88064-127-4 (pbk.)

Contents

The Ailing Empire

Introduction

If one were to view the history of the German
Reich as though through a telescope, three features would immediately come into view.

To begin with, there is the short duration of
that Reich. Its existence as a legitimate political
entity spanned a mere seventy-four years—from
1871 to 1945. Even if one were to be generous and
add the years of its forerunner, the North German
Confederation, as well as the brief post–World War
II period of the joint Allied administration of Ger-

1

many as a unit, we still would not come up with more than eighty or eighty-one years—1867 to 1948—a long life for a human being, but a mere moment in time for a state. No other example with so brief a life comes to mind.

Second, looking at that Reich, we find that it underwent radical changes both in its internal structure and its foreign relations during that short life: the two most recent upheavals before World War II took place in 1918 and 1933, respectively, and before that, another one occurred back in 1890. And so we find that within a span of eighty years Germany experienced four periods of profound change.

And finally, the third striking feature of this brief history is the role war played in it. It was given impetus by three wars and came to an end in two catastrophic world wars, the second more or less the product of the first. The history of the German Reich thus may properly be called a history of warfare, and it might not be too farfetched to assert that the German Reich was an empire built on war.

What, we may ask ourselves, accounts for a history such as this? Were the Germans inherently more belligerent than other nations? Not necessarily. Looking at their more than thousand-year-old history, we find that up to the time of Bismarck they had been involved in very few wars, and of those only a few were wars of aggression. Germany has been situated in the center of Europe since the

2

beginning of the modern age. There it formed a large, amorphous buffer zone which others frequently penetrated, and it also experienced major internal conflicts: the Schmalkaldic War, the Thirty Years' War, the Seven Years' War. . . . But unlike Germany's two ventures in our time that ultimately spelled its ruin, these earlier conflicts were internal ones, not aggressive foreign wars.

What *was* the essential cause of Germany's fall? Why did it turn into an expansionist, aggressive state, something its founder, Bismarck, had not intended? Theories about reasons abound; none of them strikes me as convincing.

One of these theories lays all the blame on the Prussians. The German Reich had after all been founded by Prussia, and its founder did indeed look upon it as a sort of Greater Prussia, as establishing Prussian hegemony in Germany. And at the very moment of its founding, the first division of Germany, Austria's expulsion from Germany, was taking place. Is Prussia then to be blamed for everything? Would events have taken a more benign course if the Frankfurt Parliament convened in 1848 had established Germany on a democratic basis?

Oddly enough, the answer is no. Contrary to what many believe, the assembly at Frankfurt's St. Paul's Church was anything but peaceful in its approach to foreign affairs. In fact, the men gathered there contemplated a number of wars: the left visualized a war against Russia to liberate Poland; the center and the "right" favored a war against Denmark over Schleswig-Holstein. And in 1848 Prussia actually did briefly wage a war over that very issue. Beyond that, we have many pronouncements by prominent statesmen in that assembly, Liberal Democrats, who asserted frankly that what they were after was power for Germany. "The German nation is fed up with principles and doctrines, with literary preeminence and a life devoted to theory. What it wants is power, power, power: And he who gives it power will be held in esteem, in greater esteem than he dreams of." Those words were spoken by Julius Fröbel, a man now forgotten but a then prominent exponent of the idea of a Greater Germany.

The men gathered in the Paulskirche all yearned to slough off the centuries of passivity that had marked Germany's existence in the heartland of Europe. They wanted to be admitted to the arena of power politics, to become expansionist, in the time-honored tradition of marginal European powers. Bismarck himself did not feel that strongly about these issues. After 1871 he called Germany a saturated state. And on the whole he was right: within the framework of that Reich, *Prussia* was indeed saturated, having spread beyond its natural areas of influence into southern Germany. Only *after* Bismarck did it become apparent that Germany was not really saturated— and precisely to the degree to which it became less and less a Greater Prussia and more and more a national state. Putting the blame on Prussia thus does not explain the guilt of the German Reich, if, indeed, guilt is to be assigned. On the contrary: as long as Prussia was preeminent it served as a brake, not as a driving force, within the German Reich.

There is no dearth of explanations for Germany's expansionism and subsequent decline. According to one theory the culprit was the rapid industrialization that transformed Germany into a major European economic power, which in turn set in motion dynamic social forces. Yet industrialization was not confined to Germany. In the nineteenth century the Industrial Revolution cut a swath through all of Europe. It made inroads into France and smaller West European countries like Holland and Belgium before coming to Germany. After Germany came Austria, and then Russia. It was a process that eventually enveloped all of Europe. Germany's industrialization did indeed proceed energetically and efficiently, but on the whole it kept step with the rest of Europe. If industrialization is to be held responsible for Germany's remarkable dynamism and expansionist tendencies, then the question arises: Why Germany? Is modern historicism perhaps attempting to establish a more intimate link between economics and politics than is warranted?

It would appear that some of the explanations are grounded in specific ideological-political views and seek to buttress those views. If one agrees with

Lenin, for example, that imperialism represents the highest form of capitalism, then capitalism must of course be held responsible for Germany's turn toward imperialism and for her ultimate collapse. I have never found this line of reasoning convincing, possibly because I am not a Marxist. But even if I were to accept the Marxist position, I would still have to admit that many capitalist states have never become imperialistic—not Switzerland, that bastion of capitalism, to name but one. Why? I have an altogether different explanation, and I believe a far more compelling one.

Switzerland is a minor state. Small powers do not have the same foreign-policy agendas as do big powers. The minor state seeks rapprochement or neutrality. It cannot hope to improve its position through independent power politics. Not so the major players. When they find an opening they move in, strengthening and expanding their power, the very basis of their existence. Unlike the earlier German governmental structures, the German Reich was a major power, and that essentially defined the difference between it and its past. However, it found very few areas open to penetration and expansion.

According to David Calleo, a young American historian, the German Reich was surrounded from birth. That is true insofar as that all along it was encircled by other major powers. To the west it bordered on France and England, to the south and southeast on Austria-Hungary, then still a significant power, and to the east on the huge Russian empire.

The geographic situation of the Reich was not advantageous. There were no areas open to penetration. This did not hold true for England and France, nor even for Belgium, Holland, Spain, and Portugal, all of which bordered on oceans, nor for Russia, with Asia to its east. Yet on the other hand, Germany had become a major power, and like other such powers it instinctively sought to become bigger still, an instinct apparently bestowed at birth. And there was yet another factor: its awkward shape. Even though from the very beginning it was probably stronger than any single major European power, it was weaker than a coalition of some of these, and certainly weaker than a coalition of *all* its immediate neighbors. That is why it always feared such arrangements. Precisely *because* France, for example, or Austria or Italy, or perhaps even Russia, felt weaker than the German Reich, these countries tended to invite alliances and form coalitions. And again, *because* they did, the German Reich always tried to prevent such coalitions, to pry connecting links loose, by war if necessary. We must keep in mind that at the time the great powers still considered war the ultima ratio, the ultimate and weightiest political instrument. As a result, the Germans—I repeat it here and subsequently will demonstrate in greater detail that they did so against the wishes of the Reich's founder—tended to consider the founding of the Reich as incomplete. They did not see it as the final step in their national history but as the springboard for a never clearly defined expansion.

Why was the German state founded in 1871 at Versailles dubbed "German Reich" rather than simply "Germany"? Probably because even then it was both more and less. It was less, a "Lesser Germany," because it excluded many Germans in adjacent areas, a nation-state only insofar as it was in Prussia's power to form such a state and insofar as it was compatible with Prussian hegemony. It was, so to speak, Prussia's German Reich.

But just as the name "German Reich" obscured this lesser factor, it hinted at the "more"— namely the European, supranational claim to universality put forth by the medieval Holy Roman Empire of the German nation.

"German Reich" could mean either as much of Germany as Prussia could dominate or as much of Europe and of the world as Germany could dominate. The former was Bismarck's interpretation, the latter, Hitler's. The road from Bismarck to Hitler is both the history of the German Reich and the history of its collapse.

And that is the uncanny aspect of this story: that the German Reich seems to have propelled itself toward its own destruction almost from its inception. Its increasing, and increasingly ill-defined, assertions of power created a host of enemies who brought it to its knees and ultimately divided it among themselves. Yet once that division had taken place, those enemies suddenly ceased to be enemies. Today the two German states that in 1949 replaced Bismarck's Reich—the Federal Republic in the West and the GDR in the East—no longer have enemies. We now find that the East is beginning to take a positive interest in the continued existence of the Federal Republic, and the West in that of the GDR. At any rate, the demise of these now forty-year-old states does not appear imminent. And that is precisely why we can now look back on the epoch of the German Reich as though through a telescope, something that was not possible before.

1

The Genesis of
the German Reich

I T IS GENERALLY ASSUMED
that the German Reich was founded in 1870–71,
but actually this is misleading. The German Reich
was not "founded" suddenly, out of the blue.
Rather, it had a comparatively long-drawn-out
genesis, spanning a period of more than twenty
years, from 1848 to 1871.

The Reich grew out of a lopsided alliance between Prussian policy in Germany on the one
hand and the German National movement on the

other. It was an unbalanced alliance not only because Bismarck weighted it toward Prussia, but also because from the very beginning it was a paradoxical, unpredictable coalition of disparate forces.

Both Prussia and the German National movement were very recent phenomena in German history. Prussia did not attain statehood until 1701, did not become a great power until the Seven Years' War of 1756–1763, and did not become a major *German* power until the Congress of Vienna of 1815. Up to that time Prussia had always leaned toward Poland, and for ten years, from 1796 to 1806, it came close to being a binational state, partly German and partly Polish. At the time Warsaw belonged to Prussia.

Not until 1815 was Prussia, turned westward, pushed into Germany, losing a major portion of its Polish possessions in the process. In compensation it received a massive western German area, the Rhineland, even though that region had no common borders with the main Prussian land area to the east. Consequently, Prussia became a geographically scattered state seeking to consolidate itself in Germany. At the same time it became the second major German power after Austria. Strangely enough, the Prussia that dominated German political life in the nineteenth century did not come into being until 1815.

The German National movement itself was not much older. It arose in the Napoleonic era.

We must remember that before the nineteenth century there was no such thing as a German state. The Holy Roman Empire had never been a nation-state, and by the thirteenth century it had begun to divide into separate states. Germans accepted this situation for what it was. In his introduction to Schiller's *History of the Thirty Years' War*, Christoph Martin Wieland wrote at the end of the eighteenth century that "it can be said with some justification . . . that the advantages that accrue to us from this division far outweigh the disadvantages, or rather that it is due precisely to it [the division] that we owe these advantages." At the time no one believed that Germany had to become a coherent power structure, a state, a national entity like France.

The National movement, and Prussia as a predominantly German great power, did not make their appearance in German history until the beginning of the nineteenth century, and initially not as allies but as adversaries. Two factors account for their hostility. First, in terms of contemporary political terminology, Prussia was "rightist," a largely feudal agrarian state ruled by a rural nobility and a modern, absolutist bureaucracy. Both these would today be called "rightist."

The German National movement, on the other hand, was a "leftist" movement. From the very outset it modeled itself on revolutionary France, hence its original ties to libertarian, liberal-democratic movements. It gained momentum after Napoleon. The Germans, at first mainly statesmen and intellectuals and later the population as a whole, reacted to Napoleon in contradictory fashion. On the one hand there was the feeling "We must never again let this happen to us," and on the other, "We too can one day do something like this." Napoleonic France became the model for the German National movement, and Napoleon its illegitimate father.

At the same time the German National movement was also an anti-French movement, because the French appeared not only as models and modernizers but also as conquerors, subjugators, and exploiters. The Germans bled profusely in the Napoleonic wars in which they reluctantly fought.

These contradictory emotions—deep-seated hatred of the French, and wistful envy—were widespread. Napoleon obviously owed his success to the nationalization and politicization of France in a revolution he had inherited and had not reversed. Even before Napoleon, the new French freedom and equality, its national democracy, had found admirers in Germany. And the German military also had its champions—officers such as Count Gneisenau and General von Scharnhorst—who said that Germany must learn from France, must imitate the French, if only to repay them in equal coin. Hatred and respect were thus intermingled.

Even now the German National movement has its grudging admirers. To this day, the early

German Nationalists, especially the highly regarded Baron vom Stein, are looked upon as outstanding German statesmen. But perhaps such judgments are too rash. Goethe's repudiation of the National movement, and Thomas Mann's treatment of that repudiation in his *Lotte in Weimar*, should allow some doubts. In this early National movement, with its hubris and self-congratulation—the notion of Germans as the one true *Volk*, the only and best in Europe; and the implacable hatred heard in Heinrich von Kleist's "Kill them! The Day of Judgment does not ask for reasons"—we can detect a whiff of the future National Socialism. And in the poetry of Ernst Moritz Arndt we find a dubious amalgam of Francophobia and a longing to imitate France. In the works of philosopher Johann Gottlieb Fichte, these sentiments seem even more extreme because of Fichte's apparent rationalism.

These trends take on special significance because, Bismarck notwithstanding, the German National movement ultimately proved to be the stronger partner in the skewed Prussian-Nationalist alliance that gave rise to the German Reich. In the final analysis, that movement rather than the Prussian sector was largely responsible for the extreme forms of German nationalism and expansionism that reached their apogee under Hitler. The "right-left" conflict was in fact only one of two reasons for the hostility between Prussia and the National movement. The origins of that conflict go back to the differences between Austria and Prussia. The National movement envisioned a Greater Germany; Prussia, on the other hand, was ready to settle for a Lesser Germany. None of this was obvious, however, before 1848.

Between 1815 and 1848 Prussia and Austria worked hand in glove, particularly in the suppression of the German National movement. Their joint instrument was the German Confederation.

At the Congress of Vienna both the revolutionary idea of a German national state and the restoration of the Holy Roman Empire had been rejected. The German Confederation, a loose union of thirty-eight states and city-states, replaced the empire that had been dissolved in 1806. The avowed purpose was to prevent the emergence of a nation-state as a power base in the middle of Europe.

The confederation was a very uneven structure, composed as it was of two great powers, Austria and Prussia; four medium-sized kingdoms, Bavaria, Württemberg, Saxony, and Hanover; and the rest, small states and free cities—almost a microcosm of the United Nations. And just as President Roosevelt, the spiritual father of the United Nations, envisioned a constant interchange of ideas between the United States and the Soviet Union, so Metternich, the father of the German Confederation, was convinced that this structure could function only if Austria, the dominant power, worked judiciously together with Prussia, the other major power. Thus the "Carlsbad Decrees" of 1819, with their provisions for muzzling the "demagogues," had been issued in Carlsbad by Austria and Prussia before being approved at Frankfurt by the German Confederation. The idea was Austria's, but Prussia played a very active role in its implementation.

The major casualties of the repressive decrees were the universities, the writers, and the press, but their real target was the National movement, to which these "media," as we would say today, lent momentum and vitality between 1815 and 1848. Consequently, the revolution of 1848 was not only a response to suppression and persecution but also a national revolution, an attempt to abrogate the decrees of 1815 and to replace the German Confederation by a German Reich, a Greater German Reich.

This first German Reich lasted for almost a year, from the summer of 1848 to the spring of 1849. It had a head of state, a cabinet, and a parliament in the form of the Frankfurt Paulskirche assembly. It was even recognized by the United States. However, it lacked a valid power base. It derived its power from the March 1848 revolution in the German states, and that revolution was not very robust. By the summer it began to run out of steam, and by the fall it had been overturned in the two major German states—bloodily in Austria and bloodlessly in Prussia. The National Assembly in Frankfurt realized that their state lacked two essentials: an army and a bureaucracy. What to do? They came up with an ingenious solution— to "borrow" these institutions—and from Prussia, of all places.

When the new German Reich decided to go to war with Denmark over Schleswig-Holstein in 1848, it charged the Prussian army with that task, and at first they had success. (This was in the early summer of 1848, when Prussia still had a revolutionary government.) But when Prussia, in response to the intervention of other powers, withdrew from that war in September and unrest broke out in Frankfurt, the Prussian army was once more called on for help. Finally, in the spring of 1849, at the close of its founding session, the Frankfurt Assembly, albeit with a slim majority, elected the Prussian king as German emperor. He refused the honor. He wanted no part of the revolution.

His refusal came as an unwelcome surprise to the men at Frankfurt. But what had been still more startling (even to themselves) was their very offer of the emperor's crown to the King of Prussia. The German National movement had always had a Greater German orientation, and the mood of the Frankfurt diet was overwhelmingly Greater German. They had installed a Hapsburg archduke as regent. Austrians were very heavily represented in the government; the Austrians had cast their votes in that assembly. Why did they now fall back on Prussia? Because it was an emergency solution, a retreat, a capitulation to the reality that, contrary to expectations, the Austrian empire had not collapsed. As a matter of fact, it flourished and had no intention whatsoever of handing over *its* Germans to a newly created German Reich. That is why they settled for a Lesser Germany under Prussian auspices. It was a piece of realpolitik on the part of the National Revolutionaries, a painful concession. But worst of all, it was a rejected concession. Still, it was the first time that the German National movement even considered a substitute solution, a Prussian Lesser Germany. Thus, long before Bismarck ever appeared on the scene, the German National movement itself gave thought to such an alliance of expediency.

This, however, was not the only instance of such a short-lived Prussian-German agreement, for immediately after the 1848 revolution Prussia took the initiative, despite its refusal of the German imperial crown tendered by the revolution. The idea of a Lesser German entity under Prussian aegis certainly did not fall on deaf ears in Berlin. There was the notion of a league of princes, loose, to be sure, yet federated, with a parliament—but of course without revolution. And so in 1849 Prussia, under Frederick William IV, created the new German Confederation, a union of 28 German states, not quite as large as the later German Reich, because Bavaria and Württemberg did not join in, and also because the Hanoverian and Saxonian kingdoms subsequently defected.

What made this move so remarkable was that the rump Frankfurt National Assembly met at Gotha and agreed to cooperate with the German Confederation. They declared that the goal pursued at Frankfurt—a German entity, if need be even a Lesser Germany—was more important than the form. The new German Confederation disintegrated, but not because of the democratic Nationalists. We must look elsewhere, to the outside, for the reasons. Austria, supported by Russia, strongly opposed this undertaking, even threatened war, and demanded the restoration of the old German Confederation. And Prussia acceded, with Bismarck delivering the decisive address in the Prussian Chamber of Deputies. At the time Bismarck still opposed the alliance with German Nationalism, supported the restoration of the old confederation, and favored the resumption of good relations between Prussia and Austria. That was why in July 1851 he was sent to Frankfurt as the Prussian representative of the resurrected German Confederation. And he stayed there until March 1859. It was during this period that Bismarck had a change of heart and decided to seek an alliance between Prussia and the German National movement.

In the following pages Bismarck will be discussed at greater length. But before turning to the story of his life, one thing must be made clear, namely that Bismarck's successful effort to forge a paradoxical alliance between Prussia and the

German National movement—an undertaking begun in 1866 and brought to fruition in 1870—was not his first such move. He had, briefly and successfully, done it once before.

The German Confederation of 1849–50 foreshadowed the German Reich of 1870–71, and in fact it resembled Bismarck's North German Confederation of 1867. With the acquiescence and cooperation of the German Nationalists and parliamentarians, the German Confederation succeeded in excluding Austria and in bringing together all of North Germany in a league of princes under Prussian aegis. Thus even the question of which member of the alliance between Prussia and the National revolution would predominate was being decided along Bismarckian lines. In 1848–49, when the revolution had still sought to use Prussia, it met with rejection. The alliance was accepted at Gotha in 1849–50 only after Prussia succeeded in pushing through a *Prussian* German policy toward the revolution. The alliance collapsed because of flaws in its foreign-policy apparatus and inadequate military preparedness, failings Bismarck was to remedy in 1866 and 1870. Therein, and basically *only* therein, lies his personal contribution to the founding of the Reich. The idea had existed before him; he had to be persuaded and converted to it.

His conversion took place in his Frankfurt period, in the 1850s, and what brought it about was his experience with Austria's policy in the restored confederation. In 1855 he wrote in a report to Berlin: "I certainly was not in principle opposed to Austria when I arrived here four years ago, but I would have had to renounce every drop of Prussian blood if I were to have preserved an even moderate liking for the kind of Austria favored by its present rulers."

We must remember that between 1815 and 1848 the German Confederation was directed under a sort of Austrian-Prussian condominium. Without a doubt Austria was not only the stronger but also the ruling power in that confederation— yet Prussia *was* the other great power. After 1815, Austria under Metternich was determined to work together with that other great power. After 1848, however, that was no longer the case. Even the resurrected German Confederation was imposed on Prussia against its will; the two powers entered into the new confederation as competitors, as rivals, as adversaries—with Austria initially being the stronger of the two.

The German National movement had been suppressed until 1848, but after that it was no longer possible to suppress it completely, because in the interval the Germans had glimpsed, however fleetingly, the real possibility of a German Reich. It was an experience they were not likely to forget. So, even though powerless, the German National movement became a political force to be reckoned with, one that either Austria or Prussia would have to harness. In 1848–49 a brand-new factor emerged, namely the "German question." And the lesson Bismarck learned during his years as Prussian delegate at Frankfurt was that as far as the German question was concerned, Austria and Prussia were rivals.

And not only Prussia but Austria was forced to formulate a German policy after 1848, and it did so in its own fashion. The very nature of the problem limited Prussia's German policy to a Lesser Germany, at times even to merely a Northern Germany; but Austria, if it hoped to remain a multinational state yet still emerge as the dominant power in a somehow united Germany, had to aim for a sort of "super-Greater Germany"—a "Reich of 70 million," as Prince Schwarzenberg, an Austrian Bismarck, said in 1850. Although Schwarzenberg died unexpectedly in 1852, his ideas, and his tendency to see Prussia as a rival that must be weakened and, if possible, destroyed in the struggle for Germany, survived. Bismarck, a prickly man, was well aware of this, even if Austria's German policy was not as outspokenly aggressive as during his Frankfurt days. In a memorandum in 1856 Bismarck wrote: "Given the policy of Vienna, Germany is too small for both of us. As long as an honest arrangement for the influence of each in Germany is not made and carried out, both of us plow the same contested field, and Austria remains the only state to which we can lastingly lose and from which we can lastingly profit." Elsewhere in that memorandum he says, "In the not too far future we will have to fight with Austria for our life, and it is not in our power to prevent it, because the course of events in Germany permits no other way out."

It is not surprising that in what one might call Bismarck's process of conversion, which lies at the root of so much of German history, hostility toward Austria ranked first. The idea of a Prussian alliance with the German National revolution, the inevitable product of this new Prussian-Austrian enmity, came later. In a long memorandum of 1858 (which Berlin's governing circles sarcastically referred to as "The small book of Mr. von Bismarck") we find this passage: "The Prussian interests completely coincide with most of the *Bundesländer* [federated provinces], except Austria, but not with that of the *Bundesregierungen* [governments], and there is nothing more German than precisely the development of the properly understood interests of Prussian particularism." And if that still sounds somewhat fuzzy, Bismarck made himself unmistakably clear a year later: "The only reliable, lasting ally Prussia can have, if it so decides, is the German people." And a year later, in 1860, he could no longer understand "why we flinch from the idea of a parliamentary representation, be it in a confederation or be it in a *Zollverein* [customs union] parliament." (Ten years earlier he had still equated "Prussian honor" with "Prussia's staying clear of any shameful alliance with democracy.") And in January 1863,

24

three months after Bismarck became Prussian minister president and foreign minister, the Prussian representative at the Frankfurt parliament issued a policy statement in support of a parliament elected in direct, secret, universal elections.

The dramatic history of the Prussian constitutional conflict to which Bismarck owed his appointment need not be gone into here. Suffice it to say that Prussia too had a very strong Liberal-National movement. Initially Bismarck's confrontational tactics had made him very unpopular in that movement, yet in the back of his mind he had always toyed with the idea that one day he might, could, and would have to propitiate and cooperate with the Prussian and non-Prussian Liberals by fulfilling their Nationalist aspirations. In his famous first presidential address Bismarck said: "Germany does not look to Prussia's Liberalism but to its power," and "The great problems of the times are not solved by speeches and majority decisions but by iron and blood." And that is indeed how things turned out.

The one phrase remembered from that speech is the provocative "iron and blood." But what is forgotten is that this address contained an emphatic peace offering to the Liberals. The minister president reminded the deputies that the government needed the bigger army they opposed in order to gain by force the very thing they themselves wanted, namely the German national state—a state allied to Prussia, led by Prussia, though a

25

Lesser German or perhaps even merely a North German Reich. That had been Bismarck's idea all along. It may be a slight exaggeration, but an exaggeration nonetheless, to say that in Bismarck's mind the war of 1866 and the peace that followed had already been concluded in 1862, when he became Prussian minister president and foreign minister. In 1890, shortly after his dismissal, Bismarck spoke the truth when he told an interviewer: "The statesman resembles a wanderer in the woods who knows the direction of his march but not the point at which he will emerge from the forest. . . . I would gladly have embraced any solution that would have led us to the enlargement of Prussia and to German unity without a war. Many roads led to that goal. I had to take each one in sequence, the most dangerous one last. Equanimity was not my way."

At any rate, the objective was clear: the expansion of Prussia, and as much German unity as was compatible with that goal. And it was equally clear from the outset that this goal could be achieved only against Austria's will, and that to achieve it the most dangerous road, the road of war, would ultimately have to be taken. That is how the war of 1866 differed from Bismarck's two other wars, including the earlier one of 1864: that war, conducted in union with Austria against Denmark for Schleswig-Holstein, was only one of the milestones in the developing Prussian-Austrian hostility over Germany, and the initially joint and later divided administration of Schleswig-Holstein was merely another bone of contention between the two German powers. Furthermore, that war had been an improvisation; its course could not have been predicted. Before the question of Schleswig-Holstein became acute, Bismarck had hardly given it a thought.

As startling as this may seem, the same can also be said of the last and biggest of Bismarck's wars, the Franco-Prussian war of 1870–71, which gave rise to the German Reich, and which, far more than the Austro-Prussian "fraternal war" of 1866, accounted for Bismarck's fame and posthumous popularity in Germany.

Let us spend a moment on this fraternal war, which revolutionized the German situation far more than the war of 1870–71. In four respects it brought much closer the goal toward which Bismarck had worked for so long via so many routes.

First, there was the vast expansion of Prussia. An entire kingdom—Hanover—in addition to Schleswig-Holstein, Electoral Hesse, and Hesse-Nassau, became Prussian provinces, and the old Free City of Frankfurt, the old seat of the German Confederation, became a Prussian provincial city. Prussia simultaneously achieved both its last and greatest expansion, and for the first time in its history won a completely contiguous German area. It would not be unfair to Bismarck to conjecture that for him as a Prussian statesman that was the most important result of the war.

Second, there was the creation of a new entity, the North German Confederation. This harmless-sounding appellation concealed the first federated German state able, and perhaps designed, to become the nucleus of the later German Reich; and four years later it did indeed become just that. The weight of the confederation's twenty-three members was very unevenly distributed: Prussia itself, after the annexation of 1866, had a population of twenty-four million, while its remaining twenty-two members had a total of six million. Still, the North German Confederation had a parliament elected by universal suffrage, a chancellor, and an army of which the Prussian army was only a part, albeit the largest by far. From Bismarck's vantage point the North German Confederation was his down payment to the German Nationalists and to their democratic-parliamentary aspirations. Whether or not Bismarck ever contemplated anything more than this first payment remains an open question.

Third, for the first time in their history four completely independent, sovereign South German states (Bavaria, Württemberg, Baden, and Hesse-Darmstadt) were connected to Prussia by military agreements and a customs union. Their union with the North German Confederation was the only internal German change wrought by the war of 1870–71. Basically this was not a great change, but in the eyes of the German Nationalists that union became the cornerstone of the Reich. At any rate it paved the way for renaming the North German Confederation the "German Reich," and making its Prussian ruler the "German Emperor."

Fourth, Austria, for the first time in a thousand years, no longer had any official ties to the rest of Germany, and therefore found itself forced to a major internal readjustment, the "settlement" with Hungary that transformed the Austrian empire into the Austro-Hungarian dual monarchy. By carefully shunning any extraneous demeaning demands for territorial concessions or reparations, Bismarck's peace with Austria left open the door to a future alliance.

From Bismarck's Prussian vantage point these developments were the ideal German condition. From the vantage point of German—even Lesser German—Nationalists, this could only be a temporary solution. But it was Bismarck and not the German Nationalists who made day-to-day German policy. And here we must ask ourselves: Did Bismarck in the years of 1867 to 1870 really contemplate the national war of integration? The Bismarck of the 1890s, the writer of memoirs working on his legend, knew how to create this impression. But if one reads what he actually said in those years, and particularly if one compares it with what he said before 1866, a different picture emerges. And the difference is striking. Before 1866 we find unswerving singleness of purpose, including a willingness to resort to extreme measures, but between 1866 and 1870 he sounds more temporizing, more mollifying or soothing. Although the Bismarck of that period was still the ally of the German National movement, one could now sense more strongly than before 1866 that he harbored reservations, most of all in the crisis of 1866 itself. In July, after the battle of Königgrätz, and before the truce of Nikolsburg, Bismarck sent the following instructions to the Prussian ambassador in Paris:

"Our Prussian requirement is limited to the disposition of the North German forces in any form whatsoever. . . . I utter the word North German Confederation without reservation because, if the necessary consolidation of the confederation is to be achieved, I consider it impossible to draw the South German–Catholic element into it. The latter will not willingly let itself be governed from Berlin for a long time still." And in a telegram to the commander of the Prussian army of the Main, Bismarck used the harsh phrase "Nationalist swindle" often heard from him before 1851, but very uncharacteristic of the Bismarck of 1866.

These words never passed his lips again. The chancellor of the North German Confederation carefully refrained from allowing anyone to raise doubts about his Nationalist German orientation, but equally carefully refrained from making any promises. For example, again writing to his French ambassador in March 1867, he said: "They wanted to erect the Main line as a wall between us and South Germany, and we accepted it because it corresponded to our needs and our interests, but could they have been so deluded as to believe that it was not a real wall but . . . a grid through which the Nationalist stream would find its way?" Or, temporizing still more, in May 1868:

"We all carry national unity in our hearts, but for the prudent politician necessity takes precedence over desirability, that is, first the completion of the building and then its expansion. If Germany were to achieve its national goal still in the nineteenth century I would consider it something great, and if it occurred in ten or even five years, it would be something extraordinary, an unexpected gift by the grace of God."

Finally, there is the perhaps most frequently quoted of Bismarck's admonitions to the German Nationalists, in an executive order to the North German ambassador in Munich of February 26, 1869: "That German unity could be promoted by force I think is probable. But it is an entirely different matter to precipitate a powerful catastrophe, and the responsibility for choosing its time. The arbitrary intervention into the evolution of history based solely on subjective factors invariably results in the plucking of unripe fruit, and that German unity at this time is no ripe fruit is in my opinion obvious."

These words clearly contradict the assertion that Bismarck conducted the war of 1870 and the war of 1866 in order to complete the process of German unification and to turn the North German

Confederation into the German Reich, even if this belief was commonly held in Germany and retrospectively given credence by Bismarck himself. Bismarck was in no hurry to "expand his house," and the crisis of July 1870 that led to war took even him by surprise. His famous "Ems telegram," which provoked France into declaring war, was an answer to France's overreaction to an already retracted proposal for a collateral Hohenzoller candidate for the Spanish throne. True, Bismarck was the author of this move, but did he really intend a war with France? Was it not perhaps a sort of test, perhaps even, to use Bismarck's words, a peace opening? For if there was bad blood between France and Prussia in the years 1866–70, it was on the part of France rather than Prussia. France felt itself short-changed, taken in, by the outcome of the war of 1866.

In 1866 Bismarck worked hand in hand with the France of Napoleon III. Napoleon III for his part pursued a policy of alliances with all European national movements—first in Italy, then in Germany, and also, unsuccessfully, in Poland. Naturally, all these alliances were to be formed under French aegis, and of course Paris expected to be rewarded territorially. These compensations were the real bone of contention between France and the North German Confederation in the four years from 1866 to 1870. By ceding Nice and Savoy, Italy compensated France fairly for the help rendered in Italy's unification (and that help was greater than that given Prussia). Bismarck also had given France hope for some modest compensation, once in 1867 in the case of Luxembourg, but then he stepped back, which explains the growing bad feeling in France, the slogan "revenge for Königgrätz," the growth of a sort of war party. Thus when, with Bismarck's connivance, a member of the Prussian royal house appeared as a candidate for the Spanish throne, the intention may have been inflammatory or diversionary or moderating. The truth will never be known. But one thing is certain: The German National question had nothing to do with the Franco-German affair of honor that provoked the war of 1870.

Be that as it may, the war with France became the first true German national war, and in the German national consciousness the subsequent expansion of the North German Confederation became the true "founding of the Reich." In 1870 German Nationalism returned to its origins: the Napoleonic era. Again France was the enemy, again there was an emperor named Napoleon, and German Nationalists in Prussia, North Germany, and South Germany saw 1870 as the revenge for the Napoleonic wars of conquest in the early part of the century. National pride and hatred of France once more rose to the surface—except now the Germans were in command. Everything was wonderful, that was how things were meant to be, and now Germany once and for all had to be consolidated as a state. That was the popular mood to which Bismarck acquiesced.

Strangely enough, he did not give in completely. This man who prior to 1866 had ruthlessly annexed North German states and deposed their monarchs, who had pulled in the reins of the smaller states of the North German Confederation, suddenly conducted himself like a statesman of the Metternich era. He negotiated patiently and at length with the king of Bavaria and the king of Württemberg, with the archduke of Baden and the duke of Hesse-Darmstadt, and he made important concessions to them. All of them were allowed to retain a certain measure of sovereignty. Bavaria was even granted real independence: a far-reaching system of taxation, its own postal service, railroad system, and army (subject to the German emperor only in time of war), and most remarkable of all, the right to its own foreign embassies and diplomatic corps. The British historian A. J. P. Taylor has said that Bismarck was the Reich preventer rather than the Reich founder, the man who allowed only as much national unity as was absolutely essential. And in fact, in its structure Bismarck's German Reich, far more than the North German Confederation, was federative rather than national.

Even though in founding the Reich Bismarck was still ready to come to terms with the Nationalists and to satisfy their emotional needs, he did not share their goal of turning Germany into the dominant and primary power in Europe. That was to become obvious during his governance of the newly formed German Reich. Now as before, he wanted to see Prussia as the dominant German power, but in the Reich this was not quite as self-evident as it had been in the earlier North German Confederation. On the contrary, once all the Lesser German hopes had been fulfilled, a Greater Germany was the next, so to speak natural, national goal.

If one contemplates that the history of the German Reich led to a situation in which, in its last and most expansionist period, an Austrian became Germany's chancellor; that this last chancellor turned Bismarck's Lesser Germany into a Greater Germany; that this Greater Germany pursued an aggressive, expansionist policy diametrically opposed to Bismarck's; and that all this was greeted by an outpouring of enthusiasm unrivaled in Bismarck's Lesser Germany, even in 1870, one is tempted to say that Bismarck's greatest triumph, the founding of the German Reich, already contained the seeds of its collapse.

2

The Bismarck Era

AT FIRST GLANCE THE forty-three years between the war of 1870–71 and World War I appear to be a harmonious era, a time when Germany's boundaries and constitution underwent no changes and neither war nor revolution disturbed the peace. These years are the longest uninterrupted period of stability in the history of the German Reich. Yet on closer inspection we find that these forty-three years are in fact two distinctive periods: the Bismarck era up to 1890, and the Wilhelmine or Imperial era after 1890. One might say that during the Bismarck era domestic policy was largely disorganized and discordant and foreign policy highly circumspect and peaceful, whereas in the Wilhelmine era it was the reverse. Domestically it was a time of much-needed reconciliation, but the foreign policy was rashly adventurous and ultimately led to catastrophe. There is no denying, however, that this very foreign policy enjoyed overwhelming popular support.

Once the elation about the victory over France and the creation of the Reich had begun to simmer down, the mood in the Bismarck era was not overly optimistic, whereas in the Imperial age it was, at least until the outbreak of World War I. In part the reason was economic. After the crash of 1873 and even beyond the Bismarck era, until 1895, the European economy, Germany's included, was stagnant, while the years from 1895 to 1914 were a time of prosperity. It is a truism that, at least in non-Socialist countries, the effect of the economy on public opinion is every bit as great as that of the political situation. And it was Bismarck's bad luck to govern in years of comparative stagnation, whereas during William II's reign the economy boomed, certainly up to World War I and in some respects during the war as well. And still another factor came into play. Bismarck's era was still a time of westward migration, of a steady flow from the Prussian agrarian areas to the western industrial regions. Moreover, during the twenty years of Bismarck's rule more than a million Germans emigrated to America. After his chancellorship German emigration fell off and soon came to an almost complete standstill. Germans now were able to find work at home, and at higher wages.

All these considerations are pertinent, but they are not my real subject. The collapse of the German Reich (which, as the historian Arthur Rosenberg once said, was mortally ill from the day of birth) was not brought on by economic problems or domestic policies but by external factors and Germany's foreign relations.

Nevertheless, Bismarck's contentious domestic policies must not go unmentioned. Even though his Prussian "crisis ministry" had begun with a deep rift between the government and the Liberals, his domestic policies rested on a compromise of the Conservatives with the National Liberals. He was convinced that a genuine understanding with his opponents could be reached by first satisfying their national aspirations and then, once that was done, giving them a say in domestic affairs. Although Bismarck was a conservative monarchist, the constitutional compromise on which his Reich rested provided for a semiparliamentarian monarchy, and the political compromise he was after in founding the Reich was a working coalition of Conservatives and National Liberals. On the whole, in his dealings with the

Liberals from 1867 to 1879, the Iron Chancellor pursued a liberal course built on a conservative base. At the end he even was ready to accept one of the Liberals, the Hanoverian Rudolf von Bennigsen, into the Prussian government, possibly even as vice minister president. However, nothing came of that. Still, during his liberal period Bismarck stood by his word. What he failed to foresee was that after 1871, despite the compromise with the National Liberals, domestic reconciliation was no longer in the cards.

Concurrent with the establishment of the Reich two completely new political parties and forces appeared on the scene, and Bismarck's response to the challenge they posed was to try and stamp them out. He failed. The two groups were the Center party and the Social Democrats. One might say they were the real parties of the Reich. In Bismarck's eyes they were *Reichsfeinde*, enemies of the Reich. The reason he considered them as enemies of the Reich was their internationalism. The Center was the party of the German Catholics, and the Catholic Church undeniably was and is a supranational institution. Because the Center was strongly Rome-oriented, it was called "ultramontane"—since it looked "beyond the mountains" toward Rome.

But what made the Center so interesting and different was its success in crossing class lines. All the other German political parties were class-based. The Conservatives were the party of the nobility, the Liberals the party of the rising bourgeoisie, the Social Democrats initially purely a workers' party. The Center on the other hand was not tied to any particular interest group. It encompassed all classes. There was a Catholic nobility, even a Catholic high nobility, a large Catholic bourgeoisie, and, of course, many Catholic workers. The Center tried to integrate all these classes and to resolve their differences internally. This was something entirely new, a kind of party heretofore unknown in Germany or for that matter in Europe—a people's party. Today, of course, almost all governing parties are inclusive.

It was precisely this supraclass structure that Bismarck could not abide. He knew how to deal with class distinctions and was very conscious of his own class, the Prussian land-owning nobility. He was not averse to negotiation with other classes and class-based parties. But a party that represented no class was a state within a state, a *Reichsfeind*, and that is why in the 1870s he tried to smash them rather than deal with them as he had dealt with the Liberals in the 1860s, first opposing them and then pacifying them. In this he failed. The Center was a powerful party from the very beginning, and in the decade of the seventies, the time of the so-called *Kulturkampf*, Bismarck's war of annihilation against the Center, it continued to grow stronger.

The Social Democrats, on the other hand, were a class party, and Bismarck could understand

41

that even the working class would want to organize politically, have a voice, defend its interests. In the sixties he was on cordial terms with Ferdinand Lasalle, one of the fathers of Social Democracy, and even developed some political plans with him, though nothing came of them. What Bismarck held against the Social Democrats was not their class character but their internationalism and, even more importantly, their then still revolutionary program.

In the beginning the Social Democrats were seen as a revolutionary party, "rabble-rousers" who openly proclaimed their intention of changing society and the state. But that did not make them enemies of the state. They wanted to carry out their revolution within the framework of the German Reich. Bismarck, however, had a deep-seated aversion to revolution, dating back to 1848. He wanted a class society, a society governed by his class—in a compromise with the liberal bourgeoisie. Had the survival of the state been at stake, he might possibly have agreed to a compromise with the working class, but he feared and hated the idea of revolution.

And so, from 1878 on, Bismarck waged a relentless battle against the Social Democrats. The Anti-Socialist Law he promulgated called for the expulsion of the Socialist leaders from their homes and outlawed Social Democratic clubs, meetings, pamphlets, and newspapers. In the second half of Bismarck's rule the Social Democrats were at best semilegal, truly persecuted. True, they could campaign and run for office and sit in the Reichstag. Bismarck did not disturb these constitutional rights. But beyond that everything was forbidden. Yet in these years of persecution the Social Democrats, almost unstoppably, grew stronger with each election. That was one of the dark clouds that hovered over the Bismarck era. Bismarck could not bring the Social Democratic party to its knees, yet he never stopped fighting it; at the very end he even tried to outlaw the party and banish its leaders from the country. But nothing came of that any longer. He also tried to fight the Social Democrats with other means. The 1880s, the years of Bismarck's relentless anti-Socialist activity, were also the years in which he introduced the German social insurance programs: health insurance in 1883, accident insurance in 1884, disability insurance in 1889. Those were truly audacious programs for that time. Bismarck was hailed as the father of modern German social legislation, and in fact to this day Germany's social policies are considered exemplary. Bismarck saw these measures as part of his fight against Social Democracy. By improving the living conditions of the people, he hoped to counteract the influence of the Social Democrats. He failed. The workers liked his social programs but they would not let themselves be bribed. They remained Social Democrats.

In the second half of his tenure, after 1879,

Bismarck tried to address the economic interests of the different German classes directly. In 1879 he forged an alliance between agriculture and industry, and the introduction of protective tariffs pleased both these groups. One might say that, in almost Marxist fashion, he tried to shape the Reich along class lines as an entity, not only politically but also with regard to its social policy.

Toward the end of the Bismarck era the Reich began to develop a duality in its domestic policy that continues to this day. Special-interest groups arose alongside the political parties. The Agricultural League as the main organization of large and small landowners east of the Elbe was not formed until 1893, after Bismarck left office. But the Central Organization of German Industrialists, the voice of heavy industry, preceded it. So did the Hanseatic League of export-oriented light industry incorporating the world of finance and banking, and also the trade unions. The unions were independent of the Social Democratic party and did not espouse revolution. They fought for better working and living conditions, above all for higher wages. They too are part of Bismarck's domestic legacy.

Yet despite all these developments the popular mood throughout the Bismarck era remained glum and tense, not only because of the economic depression but also because of Bismarck's policies, and perhaps even more because of his political style. Bismarck cannot be accused of having been conciliatory and diplomatic; his victories were rarely won by charm, and the bitterness which marked his life after his dismissal was already apparent in the hour of his greatest triumph in January 1871 ("I frequently had the strong wish to become a bomb and explode, so that the whole structure would collapse," he wrote to his wife from Versailles three days after the emperor's proclamation). One is tempted to speculate that Bismarck felt even then that he had overshot the goal he had reached in 1867, that he had allowed himself to be carried away by his alliance with the Nationalists, that he had achieved something that could not work and that in the long run would prove to be untenable. The deep pessimism with which he viewed his accomplishments is unmistakable, and that letter refers to the domestic condition of the Reich as well as to its foreign relations.

His domestic battles with the parties and the Reichstag became increasingly venomous. In 1867 he was still in comparatively high spirits when he proclaimed before the (then North German) Reichstag: "Let us put Germany into the saddle, so to speak! It will be able to ride." In 1883, quoting himself dispiritedly, he retracted this earlier optimism in a letter to Albrecht von Roon: "This nation cannot ride! . . . I say this without bitterness and very calmly: I see black for Germany's future." This passage refers to the domestic, not the external situation. But externally he felt oppressed

45

by the "nightmare of the coalitions . . . that the polar direction of millions of bayonets is the center of Europe, that we stand in the center of Europe, and as a result of our geographic situation and moreover as a result of all of European history, we are the preferred targets of the coalitions of other powers" (Reichstag speech, 1882). Somebody said to him, "You have the nightmare of the coalitions," and he replied: "This nightmare will remain a very logical one for a German minister for a long time, *and perhaps forever.*"

It is, however, doubtful that Bismarck's justified fear of hostile coalitions really had only geographic and historical causes. Rather, there is every reason to believe that they were grounded in his foreign policy. Let us be clear about the vast changes Bismarck had wrought with the founding of the Reich in 1870–71, which Disraeli even then had called the German revolution. Before that time the European area inhabited by Germans was a collection of many small and medium-sized states, and two big states loosely allied with one another (and with other European powers), none of which their neighbors had much reason to fear. The German Confederation of the years from 1815 to 1866 was not threatened by any possible coalitions of European big powers and their satellites. Then suddenly that confederation was replaced by a united, big, powerful, militarized state. In place of a huge sponge or a large amorphous synthetic layer gently cushioning central Europe against the

46

surrounding powers, there now was a block of concrete—a fear-inspiring block sprouting gun barrels. And this transformation—a source of joy for German nationalists but a more questionable development as far as the rest of Europe was concerned—had come about in the course of a war in which the new German great power had shown enormous strength as well as harsh toughness. The Franco-Prussian War of 1870–71 was not conducted with the same detached restraint as was the Austro-Prussian War of 1866. With the annexation of Alsace-Lorraine in particular, Bismarck can be said to have bestowed on Germany its *Erbfeindschaft*, its "traditional enmity" with France. Bismarck himself made a little-known but remarkable statement about this. As early as August 1871 he told the then French chargé d'affaires in Berlin, who promptly passed it on to Paris: "We made a mistake in taking Alsace-Lorraine from you if [we expected] the peace to be a lasting one. Because for us these provinces are an embarrassment, a Poland backed by France." Apparently he well knew what he had done.

Why, then, did he do it? Historians are still at odds about the answer to that question. The national cry about bringing the old German Alsace annexed by France two hundred years earlier "back to the Reich" could hardly have motivated him. As far as Bismarck was concerned his new, Prussian-dominated German Reich was not identical with that ancient Reich.

Military reasons seem more compelling. The military saw the fortresses Strasbourg and Metz as keys to the new South German regions of the Reich. As a rule Bismarck did not bow to military arguments. If he did so now, it was probably because he expected a French war of vengeance—"What they will never forgive us is our victory," he was heard to say repeatedly in 1871—and therefore military arguments had to be taken into consideration. Immediately after 1871 Bismarck's nightmare probably was not so much one of possible coalitions as of a possible French war of revenge. That became clear during the first foreign crisis of Bismarck's Reich. In 1875, France, which had rapidly recovered from war and reparations, strengthened its armies. In response, Germany, at first only unofficially, took a threatening stance. The lead editorial in a Berlin paper asked, "Is War In Sight?"

Bismarck always denied that he wanted a second, preventive war against France. That may well be so. He believed he would be able to prevent a French war of retaliation through intimidation. But now something unexpected happened. England and Russia, neither of which had intervened in the war of 1870—Russia had even assumed a position of benevolent neutrality toward Prussia and the emergent German Reich—now intervened in Berlin. They declared that they could not stand idly by while France continued to be weakened. For the first time the possibility of a future war cast its shadow over the new Reich—that is, the possible coalition of France, England, and Russia. Despite all its power, the German Reich could not risk such a coalition by going beyond what had been won in 1871.

Bismarck was deeply offended. In making his threatening gestures he believed himself to be on the defensive, not the offensive, and he reacted with bitterness to the English and Russian statesmen, particularly Russia's chancellor, Prince Alexander Gorchakov. But, more importantly, after the "war in sight" crisis of 1875, Bismarck's "nightmare of the coalitions" gave way to the "nightmare" of French revenge. That was the beginning of Bismarck's active pursuit of a peace policy—one that equated the interests of the German Reich with the prevention of a war between the European big powers. And on this policy rests Bismarck's posthumous reputation. Yet it must also be noted that he did not succeed in keeping Germany out of dangerous entanglements.

Bismarck laid out the principles of his peace policy in the famous Kissingen proclamation of 1877, in which he said: "The vision I have is not of the acquisition of some territory but of a total political situation in which all powers except France need us and are deterred from forming coalitions against us because of their relationship to one another." A brief explanation about his reference to France is needed here. In 1860 Bismarck had written a letter to his mentor Leopold von

Gerlach in which he said that, despite any possible misgivings he had, the option of cooperation with France should be kept open "because one cannot play chess when sixteen squares out of sixty-four are blocked off by the house." Now he accepted this restriction as inevitable—a terrible handicap, come to think of it.

For the rest, Bismarck's policies called for many painful concessions, to wit:

1. Renunciation of all territorial expansion in Europe.

2. In connection with that, renunciation of all expansionist efforts in Germany, particularly Greater German aspirations.

3. The disavowal of all claims to the incorporation of the "unliberated" Germans excluded from the newly formed Reich, in particular of Austrian and Baltic Germans.

4. Nonparticipation in the colonial ventures of the other European powers, in the hope that this policy would focus these powers on the outside, "the periphery," and keep them from forming coalitions against the European center.

5. If necessary, active prevention of inner-European wars, even if the German Reich was not directly involved or affected. In view of the tendency of European wars to

spread beyond their borders, the German Reich was to be the stabilizing weight in Europe.

All in all, a very respectable peace policy, and one without parallel in post-Bismarckian Germany. Moreover, it was a popular policy in Germany, which cannot be said of either the *Weltpolitik* of Imperial Germany or the revisionism of the Weimar Republic, let alone of Hitler's policy of conquest. Yet even Bismarck, despite all his efforts and extraordinary political skill, could not keep his German Reich out of dangerous entanglements. In that respect the history of the Bismarck era suggests that from the very outset his Reich was a misbegotten and possibly unsalvageable creation. Bismarck's successors all made a number of avoidable mistakes, and none could have improved on the efforts he made after 1871 to preserve and consolidate a German Reich acceptable to its neighbors as a stable, perhaps even indispensable, part of the European system of states. If ultimately even he failed, perhaps the Reich was flawed from inception.

Despite much grumbling opposition, Bismarck adhered to the first of his programmatic points with iron determination. But in 1884–85 he himself temporarily violated the fourth—abstention from colonial ventures—although that did not have the same disastrous consequences as did the greatest achievement of his fifth program-

51

matic point at the Congress of Berlin in 1878, the prevention of war through crisis management. In retrospect it is clear that this launched Germany on the road to World War I.

Even though Bismarck did not embark on his colonial venture until after the adjournment of the Berlin Congress, let us examine it first, since it was merely a side issue without significant after-effects.

In 1884 and 1885 Bismarck officially made four large African areas that already contained private German trading colonies—Togo, Cameroon, German East Africa, and German Southwest Africa—German protectorates. The facts are not disputed, but historians differ on Bismarck's reasons for doing so. Hans-Ulrich Wehler in his comprehensive study has called it an example of "social imperialism." In this he can cite the authority of Bismarck himself. In January 1885 Bismarck wrote to the German ambassador in London (who disapproved of this move because of the friction it caused between Germany and England) that the colonial question had become a vitally important matter "for reasons of domestic policy." But that actually only substitutes one riddle for another. What were these "reasons of domestic policy"? Wehler offers a wealth of possible domestic motives: the increasingly severe economic depression, the public's "intoxication" with the idea of colonies as a panacea, the fear that the pool of available African areas was shrinking, the elections of 1884, and, finally, the coincidence of the colonial policy and the equally new social-insurance program—all in all, the need for a new national unifying factor in view of the waning enthusiasm over the creation of the by now ten-year-old Reich.

There is another and, I believe, more convincing reason, which Wehler mentions only in passing. According to this theory, Bismarck by his sudden turn to colonialism deliberately invited friction with England for purely domestic, even personal, reasons, namely his fear of a liberal "Gladstonian" cabinet under Emperor Frederick III. Bismarck's son Herbert allegedly gave Prince Bernhard von Bülow, then the German chancellor, a memorandum in which Bismarck said:

"When we embarked on the colonial policy, the Crown Prince was not yet ill and we had to be prepared for a long reign in which the English influence would be dominant. To prevent this, the colonial policy, which at any moment could have led to conflict with England, had to be instituted."

There exist still clearer though even less provable remarks by Bismarck along these lines. If they are genuine, then the "domestic reason" for Bismarck's sudden turn to colonialism is crystal clear: Bismarck used it preventively to buttress his own position. Before criticizing him, we must remember that he believed—and as it turned out rightly so—that the colonial fallout with England could be controlled, but that he himself—and to some extent justifiably—was irreplaceable.

Bismarck, after all, was neither a dictator nor a constitutional ruler, but a Prussian minister president and chancellor subject to dismissal. The fact that the early days of the German empire saw an almost twenty-year-long "Bismarck era" was a constitutional anomaly due entirely to the astonishing longevity of Emperor William I. As became obvious after William II's assumption of the throne, Bismarck's position depended on the good will of the emperor. In 1884 Emperor William I was already old, and it was to be assumed that he would soon be succeeded by Crown Prince Frederick, a Liberal linked to England by marriage. Frederick was influenced by his wife and made no secret of his preference for a more liberal domestic policy and a foreign policy tilting toward England. To counteract this and to make it difficult for a future emperor to replace him with a radically different chancellor, Bismarck decided to fan anti-English feelings in Germany and, so it seems to me, intentionally heated things up by his colonial policy.

This interpretation is also borne out by the fact that in the late 1880s, when contrary to all expectations the old emperor lived to be almost ninety-two and the crown prince became mortally ill, Bismarck dropped the colonial policy like a hot potato. With the threat of a German Gladstonian cabinet thus warded off and his position assured, Bismarck's interest in German colonies died down as quickly as it had flared up. Bismarck's most famous comment against colonialism was made in 1888, when he told a visiting colonial enthusiast who showed him a map of Africa and pointed to all the hidden riches there: "Your map of Africa is very nice, but my map of Africa is in Europe. Here is Russia, and here, France, and we are in the middle. That is *my* map of Africa."

Germany's "social imperialist" hopes for a place among the world powers were by no means dead; however, they really flourished only after Bismarck's departure from the scene. On the whole, Bismarck himself, despite his aberration of 1884–85, was a man of colonial restraint. He repeatedly stressed that the race for colonies and world power was not for Germany, that Germany could not afford it, that it should content itself with preserving and safeguarding its position in Europe.

Nonetheless Bismarck's Germany got into difficulties in Europe soon after the Kissingen proclamation of 1877. The slow disintegration of the Ottoman empire, and the growing pressure of its Christian, largely Slavic, populations in the Balkans to break away, had created a festering problem along Europe's southeastern borders.

The Russians supported the anti-Turkish liberation movements of the Balkan peoples for two reasons, the first ideological—namely the incipient pan-Slavic movement in Russia—and the second power-political—namely for the effect on the Russian push toward the Mediterranean. The Russians had never abandoned their efforts to gain control over the Turkish straits, to open a sea route to the Mediterranean, and at the same time to keep the British fleet, which controlled the Mediterranean, out of the Black Sea.

The Russo-Turkish War of 1877–78, in which the Russians pushed the Turks out of a major portion of their European empire and finally reached the gates of Constantinople, was brought on by a combination of ideology and power politics. That led to a European crisis. Austria vied with Russia for the right to succeed the Turks in the Balkans, and England, which did not want to let Russia into the Mediterranean, threatened to reverse the results of the Russo-Turkish war.

This put Bismarck and the German Reich into an embarrassing position. In connection with the Kissingen proclamation Bismarck had already maintained that the German Reich should become the anchor in Europe, that is to say, exercise its influence to avoid becoming involved in a European crisis not of its making and perhaps even in a war. Thus, in the interests of Germany and of peace in Europe, which he believed overlapped, Bismarck now felt compelled to intervene to prevent a major war between Russia on the one side and England and Austria on the other.

That is when Bismarck coined his famous

phrase of the "honest broker." In the context in which it was made it exemplifies Bismarck's tactful reluctance and also his slight distaste for this sort of European mediating and peace-making role. In a speech at the Reichstag in 1878 he said:

"The mediation of peace in my mind does not mean that we play the referee in divergent opinions and say, 'That is how it should be, backed by the power of the German Reich,' but rather I see our role as more modest, more that of an honest broker who really wants to see the business deal succeed. I flatter myself that we might possibly act as trusted advisers between England and Russia as I believe we already do between Austria and Russia, if they by themselves cannot arrive at an agreement."

That was a very careful way of approaching a highly sensitive task. One has the feeling that Bismarck saw himself forced, almost against his will, into a mediating role that arose out of the geopolitical situation and the growing power of the German Reich. And the consequences were indeed tragic. The Congress of Berlin of 1878 did avert the threat of war, and the settlement that was reached—which brought some dissatisfaction as well as some satisfaction to all concerned—did have a salutary effect on Europe, but it had a terrible effect on German-Russian relations. Let us go back a bit.

After the divisions of Poland, and particularly after the anti-Napoleonic wars of liberation, Prussia, much smaller and far less powerful than Russia, was closely tied to Russia and dependent on its friendship (which Russia did generously supply), yet at the same time it was very useful to Russia. That was how matters stood between these two friendly powers until 1866 and 1870. Russia gave Bismarck the backing he needed in his war against Austria and later against France when he sought to unite Germany under Prussian leadership.

Russia's actions were based on the belief that its traditional ties to Prussia would continue. The fact that in the interim the German Reich had come under Prussian control would, so Russia believed, work to its advantage. Moreover, the Russians also believed that their actions in 1866 and 1870 would entitle them to Prussia's gratitude—to a quid pro quo.

Instead of that quid pro quo, Bismarck did the very thing that he had taken such pains to avoid—and with Russian assistance—in 1866 and 1870: he made a bilateral quarrel the subject of a European congress. And at this congress Russia suffered substantial losses.

Bismarck later claimed that his role at the congress was almost that of an additional Russian delegate, and he probably wanted to ameliorate Russia's deep disappointment as much as possible. That does not alter the fact that the congress and its outcome stabbed Russia in the back. Bismarck robbed victorious Russia of some of the fruits of that victory, and furthermore brought Austria, Russia's rival in the Balkans—although it had not fought in the war—an unearned reward, namely the right to Bosnia and Herzegovina. Russia understandably was dismayed and resentful. In 1878 and 1879 anti-German and anti-Bismarckian feelings surfaced in the Russian press and in Russian diplomatic circles and even colored the relationship of the two dynasties. In 1879 an irritated Bismarck responded with a pact between the German Reich and Austria-Hungary. This represented a profound change in, almost a reversal of, the policies of 1867, when Bismarck, with Russia's backing, had ousted Austria from Germany. Now Austria was allied with Bismarck's Germany—against Russia.

Perhaps Bismarck did not look on the German-Austrian alliance as a permanent arrangement. Yet that is precisely what it turned out to be. For eventually the logical consequence of the German-Austrian alliance was a Russian-French alliance. George Kennan in his important book *The Decline of Bismarck's European Order* (1979) says that the Russian-French alliance was not an improvisation of the 1890s. It had been in the making almost unstoppably since the German-Austrian alliance of 1879. That is where it took root. Of course the status of the two alliances was still somewhat oblique. Russia had no direct conflict with Germany, nor France with Austria. However, Germany and Austria were now allied.

This gave rise to a growing tendency both in Russia and France to counter the German-Austrian alliance with a permanent one of their own.

As long as he was in power, Bismarck, with well-nigh acrobatic skill, was able to ward this off. In 1881, despite the ill feeling between Petersburg and Berlin and the enmity between Petersburg and Vienna, he still managed to bring about a sort of alliance of those three powers: the monarchic triple alliance. It took great skill and somewhat creaky, moth-eaten arguments about the need for monarchic solidarity in the face of the liberal-democratic West. This triple alliance lasted only six years. It was too artificial, too contrary to the natural flow of events. Like all of Bismarck's alliances of the eighties, it had an air of contrived virtuosity, almost of frivolity.

In 1882 Bismarck forged still another, no less unnatural alliance, namely the German-Austrian-Italian Triple Alliance. In both cases Germany became the mediator who turned two natural enemies into reluctant allies. Because of Trentino and Trieste, which belonged to Austria but which Italy considered unliberated Italian territories, Austria and Italy were as much natural enemies as were Austria and Russia because of the Turkish succession in the Balkans.

When the three-emperor alliance collapsed in 1886, Bismarck did something impermissible. Behind the back of his ally Austria he concluded a secret agreement, the so-called reinsurance pact, with Russia, which flew in the face of the German-Austrian alliance. By granting Russia supremacy in Bulgaria and pledging benevolent neutrality even in the case of a Russian conquest of Constantinople, this pact ran counter not only to the Austrian alliance of 1879 but even to Bismarck's "honest brokerage" at the Congress of Berlin. In defense of Bismarck it has been said that he concluded his pacts of the 1880s not for the reasons pacts are generally made—protection in the event of war—but rather that he pursued his deft, contradictory policy of agreements to prevent such a war.

That may be so. While in the late 1880s the German and Austrian general staffs were busy drawing up preventive war plans against Russia, Bismarck wrote to the chief of the military cabinet: "It is the task of our policy to prevent the war altogether, if possible, and if not, at least to postpone it. I could not take part in any other [policy]."

Still other completely convincing remarks by Bismarck in the late eighties could be cited to show that he really identified the interests of the German Reich with the interests of European peace. None of his successors did so with the same determination, nor does it detract from his achievement that he acted out of profound pessimism. ("If by the will of God we were to lose in the next war," he wrote in a letter of 1886 to the minister of war, "then I have no doubt that our victorious opponents will use every means to pre-

61

vent us from ever getting back on our feet, or at least in the next generation. . . . Once these powers have seen how strong a unified Germany is . . . we could not even count on the preservation of the present Reich after a failed military campaign.") Bismarck's policy was the only broad-based peace policy ever pursued by the German Reich.

Yet in his time Bismarck, granted his enormous political skill and honest intentions, did not quite reach the goal he had set himself. By his actions in the founding of the Reich he himself had created an implacable, lasting enemy for Germany —France—and his policy at and after the Congress of Berlin set the stage for a Franco-Russian alliance. At the same time he entered into an intimate relationship with Austria that, although he tried to prevent it, contained the seeds of conflicts. For unlike Bismarck's Germany, Austria was not a satisfied country. Like Russia, Austria wanted to inherit European Turkey, and this made a future conflict between Austria and Russia almost inevitable. Bismarck's Germany, despite his best intentions, became entangled in a conflict from which it was never able to disentangle itself. In 1914 this conflict of 1878–79 led directly to World War I. But in the background of World War I lay another conflict, the one between England and the German Reich, this one brought on not by Bismarck (despite his anti-English policies of 1884–85) but by the "world politics" of Wilhelm II.

3

The Imperial Age

BISMARCK'S FALL, IN March 1890, had two immediate effects, one on domestic policy and the other on foreign policy. Two major pieces of legislation were allowed to lapse—the Anti-Socialist Law and the Reinsurance Law. The effect of their expiration was not felt immediately. The relationship with Russia did not crumble right away, nor were there any perceptible changes in the government's treatment of the Social Democrats. But a great deal did change between 1890 and the outbreak of World War I, most dramatically on the domestic scene. Thus the Social Democrats turned from a revolutionary party into a reformist one.

Bismarck's Reich, as we know, was not a happy country. It was an era of political restrictions and dissatisfaction, and the economic stagnation lasted well beyond the Bismarck years. The economy did not recover until 1895, and then, except for two minor recessions, in 1901 and 1908, it remained vigorous until the outbreak of World War I. On the whole the Imperial age was a period of economic well-being and prosperity for all, including the working class. The reason continues to puzzle us, but that should not come as a surprise. After all, long-range economic forecasts are as arcane a science now as they were then.

Two eminent modern economists, Schumpeter and Kondratiev, have argued convincingly that economic recovery is linked to major innovations, and that an economy stagnates and can even go into recession in times of technical or scientific standstill. That certainly was the case in the Bismarck era after the Industrial Revolution. Production became mechanized after the introduction of the steam engine and railroads and steel and iron, and then, in the 1870s and 1880s, nothing really new appeared. Of course railroads were still being built and workers were still employed in established industries, but overall, industrialization slowed down. Eighteen seventy-three to 1895 was a time of slow starts, and it remained so until the later nineties, when another series of major breakthroughs—electrification, motorization, and wireless communications—swept the world and breathed new life into the economy.

This economic process had both social and political consequences. Socially it meant that the class struggle gradually became less intense. Even though the view that workers were not merely cost factors but also consumers had not yet penetrated, and that it therefore was in the best interest of industry to meet the unions' demands for higher wages, the growing labor shortage and the increasing power of the unions were making themselves felt. Employers were slowly beginning to discard the old iron law of keeping wages to a minimum. This change brought a modicum of social harmony, and this in turn had political consequences, primarily in the evolution of German Social Democracy.

The founding program of the SPD, the German Social Democratic party, had the unqualified support of the First International. It was a revolutionary document calling for social change. The SPD became the party of world revolution, at least in theory, for the revolution it projected was elusive, just around the corner. But revolution remained the theoretical goal of the Social Democrats until well into the nineties, despite the emergence of a faction within the party, the so-called revisionists, who believed that revolution was not necessary. Instead, they thought that the party should accommodate itself to the existing society and the state so as to be able to take it over at some future time.

This was not a majority position within the SPD. In the endless debates about revisionism in party congresses the revisionists were outvoted. However, their growing influence became apparent in 1914, when the Social Democrats came out in support of the war; and it became even more clear in 1918, after Germany's defeat, when, in the words of Friedrich Ebert, the party chairman, they declared themselves ready to "jump into the breach." These later developments attest to the relaxation of domestic tensions during the Imperial era even in the absence of any programmatic revisions. The Wilhelmine era did not have a Prussian constitutional conflict or a *Kulturkampf* or anti-socialist laws. The Reichstag and its parties took on new importance because the government depended on the Reichstag to keep the flow of new legislation moving. (The Imperial age was a period of major legal codification. Except for its family law, the Civil Law Code of 1900 has remained unchanged to this day.) It would be an exaggeration to say that it was an age of democratization, but it was an era of a politicization that laid the groundwork for a future democratization.

I mention this largely because this puts me at odds with a still popular school of German historiography that holds that the expansionist policy of the German Reich under Wilhelm II had domestic causes. Internal tensions, it is claimed, were, or even had to be, diverted toward the outside. I do not agree. Internal social and political tensions did not increase in the twenty-four-year period from 1890 to 1914. On the contrary. Moreover, it also seems to me that a comparison with other countries contradicts this view. Domestic tensions in most of the other countries at that time were much greater than in Germany. France had the Dreyfus affair, England the Irish problem, Russia the 1905 revolution, and Austria its nationality conflict. The German Reich had no such problems.

Domestically the Wilhelmine age was a happy time, perhaps the best ever in the brief life of the German Reich. What propelled the Reich on its new and, as it turned out, extremely dangerous course in its foreign relations was not internal discord and dissatisfaction but rather an overoptimistic assessment of its power and domestic harmony. All classes were prospering. Hand in hand with this went a change in the character of the German people, a change not for the better. Before 1848, and even under Bismarck, the Germans were a basically moderate people. Their highest aspiration was to live together as a nation under one roof, and that they achieved.

But after Bismarck an urge for great-power status seemed to sweep the country. People from all walks of life suddenly fell under the spell of a grand national vision, a national goal. It was as though they were telling themselves, "We shall become a world power, we will expand throughout the world, Germany will lead the world." Their patriotism took on a new aspect. What inspired them and raised their spirits was "nationalism," not so much a feeling of community as the consciousness of being somehow special, the wave of the future.

This change was also connected with the great improvement in everyday life wrought by technology and industry. It was now possible to talk over the telephone, switch on a light bulb, or even operate a sort of wireless transmitter. Undreamed-of new frontiers were opening up. In many fields the Germans were in the forefront in Europe. While things were moving forward only slowly in England and even more haltingly in France, and while Russian industrialization was still in its infancy, German technology and industry were moving forward at record speed, and Germans were filled with pride. Unfortunately, this pride often took the form of braggadocio, of overweening self-congratulation.

Like the rest of Europe Germany was of course a class society. And it is true that Bismarck's compromise of 1879, which introduced protective tariffs and forged the coalition of industry and agriculture, had put the upper classes, the big landowners and the industrialists, on an equal footing, with the landowners possibly exercising a bit more influence than their actual wealth entitled them to. In that respect it would be fair to say that Germany was somewhat backward. However, in the Imperial era this alliance of large landowners and heavy industry underwent a change. The weight now began to shift from agriculture to industry. This shift had already started under Bismarck, when Germany began to change from an agricultural country into an industrial one, but it was not until the Wilhelmine era that German industry began to make unparalleled strides, rivaled perhaps only by faraway America. And by furnishing the means for expansionism, industry might be said to have prompted the turn to the policy of expansionism, to imperialism. German foreign policy was intertwined with German industrial and commercial expansionism. Still, I do not believe that this accounts for the change in foreign policy. Rather, granted the growing consciousness of Germany's strength, the reason is to be found in Germany's reassessment, its mistaken reassessment one might say in retrospect, of the future course of the European powers.

As late as 1888 Bismarck had said that *his* map of Africa lay in Europe, by which he meant that Germany, being so hemmed in, had enough problems in Europe without going in search of adventure abroad, an opinion not shared by everyone even then. By now it had undergone a basic change.

In Europe the late nineteenth and early twentieth centuries were the years of colonial imperialism. All the powers, regardless of size, tried to expand beyond Europe, to pursue *Weltpolitik*, to become "world powers." England was the first and the most successful. The British Empire was, or at least appeared to be, an impregnable world power. But France also ruled over a large colonial empire in Asia, and even more so in Africa. As Spain and Portugal had earlier, Russia expanded eastward, and smaller countries like Holland and Belgium, and later Italy, followed suit. A seemingly irresistible and plausible idea spread throughout Europe. It held that the era of the purely European power system and balance was about to be replaced by a system of world power in which the European powers, which saw themselves as the rulers of the world, would form large colonial empires and transform the European balance into a world balance centered on Europe.

Those who shared this view—and in Germany a great many opinion leaders did—also believed that considering its industrial strength, Germany was lagging behind. True, Bismarck had founded a few African colonies (only to ignore them soon thereafter), but certainly nothing like a German world empire existed. Germany was still only a European power, not the world power it wanted to be. In 1895 Max Weber furnished the Wilhelmine age with its rationale when he said: "We must understand that the unification of Germany was a youthful prank committed by the nation in its old age and, because of the cost [of that prank], it would have done better to have left things alone if it turned out to be the end and not the starting point of a German *Weltmachtpolitik*."

In the pursuit of that policy the Reich was bound to come up against the dominant world power, England. The destruction of the British empire was never Germany's goal, neither then nor later. But Germany did want to replace the European balance of power, which was controlled by England, by a world balance in which Germany would stand beside the established colonial powers, and England would be just one power among the others. Chancellor Bülow summed this up thus: "We do not wish to put anyone in the shade, but we also want to have a place in the sun."

Strangely enough, in the Wilhelmine era the Germans did not gain all that many new overseas possessions. In the nineties they did get the very remote Chinese lease territory of Kiaochow (the lease agreement, incidentally, was not due to expire until 1987), a remarkably farsighted move since the division of China among the European great powers seemed imminent, although, as we now know, it never actually came to pass. Moreover, Germany acquired a number of South Sea islands, also very remote and hard to hold on to in the event of a conflict. Apart from that a significantly expanded German colonial empire remained a pipe dream.

But the Germans, methodical as always, convinced themselves that if Germany were to establish a position of power it needed a fleet, "command of the sea." That seemed logical. If a country wanted to become a world power, to compete and win the race for colonies, it needed the appropriate instrument, namely a fleet able to acquire and, if necessary, defend the newly won overseas possessions. By the same logic this naval policy created fresh enmity with England. England was bound to feel challenged by the creation of a large, competitive German fleet. What made this move doubly hazardous was the fact that on the continent Germany already faced a French-Russian alliance and that in the event of a future war Germany would have to fight on two fronts. Under these circumstances a rapprochement with England, which did not seem completely illusory, would appear to have been in Germany's interest.

As I mentioned earlier, as far as foreign policy was concerned, the transition from Bismarck to the Imperial era was smooth. The new naval policy was not decided upon and initiated until 1898. There was an eight-year interval in which Germany attempted to broaden and consolidate its alliance with Austria-Hungary and Italy by an alliance with England, or at least an entente (a then still unfamiliar term). This possibility was already talked about in the late Bismarck years, since the enduring differences between England and Russia contained the seeds of conflict. And as we know,

Bismarck's main objective at the Congress of Berlin in 1878 was the prevention of a war between England and Russia. In 1887 the Russo-English differences flared up again, and the so-called First Mediterranean Agreement between Austria, Italy, and England was concluded to oppose the Russians in case they once again attempted to move toward Constantinople.

It would have seemed logical for Germany to join this alliance. That would have created a coalition of Germany, Austria, Italy, and England on the one hand, and Russia and France on the other. Even then Germany might still have had to fight a two-front war, but with English backing such a war might be winnable, or at any rate the prospects more auspicious than turned out to be the case.

Bismarck shunned the alliance. He always tried to hold on to Germany's option between England and Russia, perhaps even with the idea of dropping Austria if push came to shove and resurrecting the old German-Russian friendship. He did not join the Mediterranean Agreement he had supported. On the contrary, he approached a now somewhat isolated Russia by concluding the problematic Reinsurance Treaty. However, Bismarck's successor, Leo von Caprivi, allowed this agreement to lapse, thereby removing the last, feeble obstacle to a Franco-Russian alliance, which had been in the making since 1878–79 and was made official in 1894. It thus seemed even more logical for Germany to fall back on the old idea of a Mediterranean agreement and to move closer to England.

Caprivi tried it. It is now almost forgotten that soon after taking office Caprivi concluded the German-English colonial agreement by which England got Zanzibar, and Germany, Helgoland. It was to be the beginning of closer ties between the two powers. As long as Caprivi was in office and even thereafter, efforts to strengthen the ties continued. The relationship between Germany and its allies on the one hand, and England on the other, was fairly cordial up to 1897, in the years of the so-called New Course. Relations between England and Germany were certainly not hostile. Even in 1897, when Admiral Alfred von Tirpitz, the architect of Germany's naval policy, stirred up popular feeling in support of a German fleet, which by its very nature had an anti-English thrust, Germany and England did not become estranged. On the contrary. British government officials gently tried to steer Germany away from its naval and *Weltpolitik* plans and toward European alliances. Between 1898 and 1901 there were repeated exploratory talks—they cannot really be called serious discussions—about an English-German alliance. These ultimately failed, largely because the Germans reasoned that they had England in their pocket, for if it was ready to come around when the fleet was only a plan, it would certainly be ready to make an agreement once Germany achieved greater naval strength.

It is an argument strangely similar to Konrad Adenauer's Germany policy of a much later time. In 1952, when Russia, faced with West Germany's imminent entry into the Western alliance, offered reunification in exchange for neutrality, Adenauer argued that the Russians would be willing to make still greater concessions once West Germany was stronger. It would seem that there is a recurrent tendency among German foreign-policy experts to overestimate German bargaining power and to believe that events have to follow a preordained course. They never consider the possibility of change once that which appeared only as a threat has become reality, in which case preventive conciliation might turn into hostility.

This reversal in English policy took place at a comparatively late date—the rapprochement with France came in 1904, and that with Russia not until 1907. In 1904 England more or less had settled its colonial differences with France, which toward the end of the nineteenth century had again become quite acrimonious. France's renunciation of Egypt in exchange for a free hand in the still uncolonized Morocco lay at the heart of the Franco-British colonial agreement. By moving against France in Morocco—Germany's first active intervention in a colonial affair—Germany wanted to sour the enjoyment of the two signa-

75

tories of this entente cordiale. The first Moroccan crisis of 1905, which began when Germany dispatched the kaiser to Tangiers with a guarantee of Moroccan independence from France, was the first real crisis in the long peaceful period from 1890 to 1914.

This move typified the lack of coordination in German foreign policy. In 1905 Russia was involved in a war with Japan which Russia did not win. That same year Russia had its first revolution and ceased to be a ranking European power. Subsequently, the German General Staff under Alfred von Schlieffen, who played a very important political role in Germany, began to toy with the idea of a preventive war against France. The Franco-Russian alliance appeared to be crippled, and Russia paralyzed. This prompted France to seek a rapprochement with England by concluding the colonial agreement. Using Morocco as a pretext, Schlieffen seized the opportunity to settle a score with France. By involving France in a land war in which Russia could not readily intervene and in which England could not play a decisive role, he meant to weaken France and prevent it from playing a significant part in any future coalitions of the major powers for years to come.

This plan, which originated in the General Staff, won the support of one of the most influential men in the Foreign Office, Senior Councillor Friedrich von Holstein, who persuaded Bülow, the chancellor and foreign minister, to support it. But

Bülow did not want a war. He wanted a diplomatic coup to teach the French that when things got serious they could not count on the help of either the Russian alliance or the English, and in this way perhaps make France receptive to a future coalition with Germany.

The kaiser for his part did not want any crisis at all, and certainly not a war. Despite his occasional triumphant proclamations, William II was basically a sensitive, nervous, peace-loving man. He went to Tangiers reluctantly, and later, as the crisis developed, shrank back from going further.

Bülow, nonetheless, had won a prestigious victory. The French foreign secretary resigned, and Bülow, like Bismarck after the victorious war of 1870–71, was raised to princely rank. Everything seemed under control, particularly when Germany once again organized a European conference and, just as at the Congress of Berlin, mediated the settlement of an international crisis, even if this time it was a crisis of its own making. However, things did not turn out quite as well now. The Algeciras Conference was a fiasco, a warning for German policymakers. Except for Austria, none of the great powers was ready to oppose France, and France ultimately was granted colonial control over Morocco. The Germans won only some minor face-saving concessions.

The crisis of 1905, the first of three serious prewar crises of the empire, clearly showed that Germany had overreached itself. It ushered in an

English-French-Russian coalition—the very antithesis of what Germany had had in mind. Instead of moving the Reich closer to its objective, its *Weltpolitik*, the outcome served as a rude reminder that Germany's position in Europe was by no means secure: One careless step and Bismarck's nightmare of coalitions could become reality.

Three years later an altogether different crisis occurred, and this one turned into the prelude to World War I. In October 1908 Russia, in conjunction with Austria, attempted a political maneuver to gain unobstructed passage through the Turkish Straits. Petersburg and Vienna concluded a secret agreement removing Austrian objections to Russian passage through the straits. In return, Russia promised Austria the right to the formal annexation of Bosnia and Herzegovina, both of which had been occupied and administered by Austria since 1878. However, according to the provisions of the Berlin Agreement of 1878, free passage through the Turkish Straits required not only Austrian but English and French concurrence as well. While Russia was still involved in these ultimately unsuccessful negotiations, Austria annexed Bosnia and Herzegovina. This surprise move gave rise to great tension between Austria and Serbia, a Russian client state. Serbia threatened war if Austria did not reverse its decision to annex. A major Balkan crisis erupted in the fall of 1908—posing the direct threat of an Austro-Serbian war, and, as would happen in 1914, the indirect threat of Russian intervention on the side of Serbia.

The German Reich, as a faithful ally of Austria and referee over this area of Europe, intervened. It asked Russia to call Serbia off and to recognize the annexation of Bosnia, otherwise Germany would feel called upon to put its full weight behind Austria and let events run their course. Germany, in the words of its press, stood "in shining armor" on the side of Austria against Russia and had humiliated Russia. Petersburg was forced to capitulate for the simple reason that even with the backing and support of France it was not strong enough to risk war with Germany and Austria so soon after its drubbing by Japan and the revolution of 1905. Russia pulled back. Germany had scored a diplomatic victory, but in the long run this triumph proved as futile and dangerous as the at best mixed victory over France in 1905. For Russia now saw itself forced to build up its armies as quickly as possible. It was not going to suffer another Bosnia-type setback. In the Bosnian crisis of 1908–09 Germany tested the waters of the continental war which ultimately erupted in 1914.

A second Moroccan crisis broke out in 1911. Whether or not France, in expanding into southern Morocco, violated the provisions of the Algeciras Agreement is open to question. But there can be no doubt that the dispatch of a German gunboat to southern Morocco was a threatening gesture. Again there was a confrontation with France that ultimately was settled peacefully, and once again Germany chalked up a minor gain: The French agreed to cede a small area of the Congo to Germany in exchange for German disavowal of any designs on southern Morocco. This, incidentally, was Germany's first colonial expansion in Africa since Bismarck. However, this second Moroccan crisis had more serious consequences than either the previous one or the Bosnian crisis, for now England for the first time openly entered the arena on the side of France.

Neither of the earlier English agreements, the 1904 agreement with France and the 1907 agreement with Russia, were actual alliances. The former was designed to settle overseas conflicts with France and the latter to settle conflicts with Russia (in Persia), freeing England to join a Franco-Russian coalition should the occasion arise. England had also held secret military talks with France, but no actual alliance was formed. England did not commit itself to intervene on the side of the Franco-Russian alliance in the event of a land war.

Now for the first time a British statesman, Chancellor of the Exchequer and later Prime Minister Lloyd George, delivered a sensational speech that Germany construed as a challenge, in which he said that England would not stand idly by if France were threatened. Also in that same year,

1911, the general staffs of England and France began negotiations that were more productive than those of 1904–05. The possibility of a British expeditionary force coming to the aid of France in the event of a war with Germany was given serious consideration. The clouds of war were beginning to gather.

Yet at this very time another comprehensive proposal for a German-British accord was made. It cannot be said that in 1911 any of the powers involved, least of all England, wanted a major war. But all of them were aware that the possibility existed, and they were determined to prepare for it. France introduced compulsory three-year military service, and in 1913 Germany beefed up its armies, surprisingly enough with the support of the Social Democrats. (The military expansion was financed by a capital tax, which helped win the Socialists over.) During the Bosnian crisis the Russians had already begun to rearm and to expand the strategic rail lines in Poland, to reinforce their fortifications and build up their artillery. Those, of course, were long-range plans. It was assumed that Russia would not be able to complete them before 1916–17.

Now, at the very time when everyone began to take seriously the possibility of a war between the two great European alliances, Germany and England made a last great effort to reach an understanding. Germany was interested in keeping England out of such a war, and England wanted to quell the threatening conflict with Germany. Germany hoped for a major colonial settlement similar to those between England and France in 1904 and England and Russia in 1907. Together with England the Germans were ready to define and delimit their colonial goals. This joint effort culminated in the Haldane mission in the spring of 1912.

England was primarily interested in a joint agreement to control the naval arms race. (Today the idea of arms control agreements in conflict situations is taken for granted, but at that time it was an innovative notion.) Germany's goal in the negotiations with Haldane was to win a British guarantee of neutrality in the event of a European war. Neither of them succeeded. The English were not ready to guarantee neutrality, because even then they feared that Germany would win a land war and thus solidify its plans for world power. Tirpitz, unlike Chancellor Bethmann Hollweg, was not ready to conclude a naval arms control agreement to contain German naval power. The chancellor outranked the secretary of the navy, but the kaiser, who was almost offended by this newfangled notion of arms control, came out on the side of Tirpitz against Bethmann Hollweg and checkmated the chancellor.

This doomed the Haldane mission and of course intensified German-English tension. Still, negotiations between the two powers continued in 1913 and 1914, although less overtly. A colonial settlement was discussed. Germany for the first time put its African colonial design on the table in London. It wanted to reserve the right to the possible future acquisition of the Portuguese colonies, primarily Angola and Mozambique. Portugal was believed to be bankrupt and therefore, in a manner of speaking, might have to "sell" its colonies. Moreover, Germany also stood ready to buy part of the Belgian Congo from Belgium if the opportunity offered itself and in this way acquire a contiguous land mass extending from German Southwest Africa to German East Africa, via Angola and the Congo. If these conditions were met, Germany declared itself satisfied; England also stood to gain some Portuguese and possibly some Belgian colonial possessions as well.

These negotiations, carried out in a rather friendly fashion, did yield some sort of preliminary result in June 1914, on the eve of the war. A secret agreement on the future disposition of colonial holdings in Central Africa was in the process of being drawn up in London. Thus in the very area that had given rise to the German-English conflict, the area of colonial and "world" policy, a relaxation of tension seemed possible.

Apparently promising negotiations between England and Germany were being conducted in still other areas. Since the beginning of the century German *Weltmacht* aspirations had been twofold: First there was the acquisition of large areas in Africa; and then, though at the time this was still only vaguely defined, there was expansion toward the southeast. In this second push the German-Austrian alliance together with the new German-Turkish alliance was to form a huge, unified, initially only economic, structure. The hope was to force all or a portion of the Balkan states into such a system. It was symbolized by a grandiose plan for a rail link between Berlin and Baghdad. The German Reich wanted to establish a sphere of influence between the Russian and English spheres of influence, but without being clear in its own mind how such an economic-political structure could be created and what form it ought to take. Austria still considered itself, and behaved like, a major power, and the Ottoman Empire still was an independent though declining power. The German Reich tried to strengthen its ties to the Ottoman Empire, into which the revolution of the Young Turks in 1908 seemed to have breathed new life. A German military mission in Constantinople was to train the Turkish army along German lines. At the same time the prospect of a political treaty was held out to Turkey.

That expansion was the thrust of Germany's plan was unmistakable, particularly since England also had strong interests in the southern region of the Turkish Empire, present-day Iraq. Oil had already become a factor. One of the objectives of these negotiations was to define the respective German and English spheres of interest, amicably if possible. And this too was done more or less successfully.

Consequently Bethmann Hollweg once again began to hope that in the event of a land war England would remain neutral, even though neutrality had never been promised. But then England also had never said that it was going to intervene in the event of a war. Now that some understanding had been reached in the area of colonial and expansionist policy, the settlement of old differences seemed possible. After all, that is how the entente between England and France, and later between England and Russia, had begun. Why wouldn't it be possible for relations between England and Germany to improve despite the continuing naval rivalry? Perhaps England could even be induced to act as a sort of neutral arbitrator in the event of a European war, at least in the early stages.

That was the speculation on which Bethmann Hollweg based his policy in the summer crisis of 1914. But German military planning was to render all his calculations null and void.

4

World War I

As RECENTLY AS TWENTY years ago any attempt to explore the causes of World War I was still a very touchy matter in Germany, because the focus was still on the so-called question of war guilt. In the 1920s German historiography was largely preoccupied with exonerating Germany from the charge of having played a part in unleashing the war, and even in the late 1960s it took courage for the Hamburg historian Fritz Fischer to examine Germany's role.

But thanks largely to Fischer, it is now possible to discuss this subject more candidly.

Actually, the concept of war guilt as we understand it today has no place in a discussion of the events of 1914, a time when war was still thought of as a legitimate political tool. All big powers considered the possibility of war; their general staffs were forever devising strategies, and if victory was deemed possible it was not thought immoral, certainly not criminal, to resort to war. What makes Germany's role in the outbreak of the war of interest to us is the differences in the projections of the government, particularly Chancellor Bethmann Hollweg's, and those of the German General Staff. Let us take a closer look at this aspect.

As early as 1911 the specter of war already hovered over Europe. A clash seemed likely, and in preparation for that eventuality the prospective combatants jostled for the most favorable position.

According to everything we know about his thinking in those prewar years, Bethmann Hollweg recognized the likelihood of German involvement in a future war and believed that such a war was winnable (1) if Austria was involved, (2) if the Social Democrats supported it, and (3) if England remained neutral.

In light of these projections, the situation in 1914, after the assassination of Archduke Franz Ferdinand of Austria in Sarajevo, certainly looked promising. The threatened war was not going to be a German war, but rather an Austrian war against Serbia. And if Russia were to intervene on the side of Serbia, Austria, considering that it was its war and not Germany's, was sure to seek an alliance with Germany. Moreover, the German Social Democrats in all likelihood would support a war against czarist Russia. Finally, and best of all, England probably would not intervene in a war confined to the East, not immediately at any rate. It was a logical calculation. Throughout its history England had steered clear of involvement in East European conflicts. And in this particular situation no British interests were at stake. As a matter of fact, it seemed that England might not be averse to, and perhaps even welcome, a shift in power from Russia toward Austria.

These speculations, however, were based on the assumption that militarily the war would remain what it started out as: an East European conflict between Germany and Austria on the one side, and Russia and Serbia on the other. The war, in its early stages at least, ought to have followed this course: Austria, provoked by the murder in Sarajevo, attacks Serbia; Russia comes to the aid of its client Serbia and attacks Austria; Germany comes to the aid of its ally Austria and attacks Russia. Of course Germany had to consider that in the West, France would come to the aid of its ally Russia and attack Germany. But in that event, Germany would be the victim of an attack on its western flank, and if it remained on the defensive there the British might not intervene.

These were the thoughts underlying the famous "blank check" Bethmann gave the Austrians on July 6, 1914, when he told them that in the case of war between Austria and Russia as a result of Austrian reprisals against Serbia, Austria could confidently count on the firm support of its loyal ally, Germany. However, no further explanation of what form this firm support would take was forthcoming. Taken literally it should have meant that Germany would move against Russia if Russia were to attack Austria. Had the Austrians been told in so many words that Germany would not immediately act against Russia but instead use the Austro-Russian conflict as a pretext for moving against France and Belgium, Vienna possibly might not have gone to war. However, it did.

The war plan of the German General Staff did not concern itself with the political center of the crisis that gave rise to the war. Their plan called for a march through neutral Belgium to allow a lightning strike against France. The General Staff believed (probably rightly from a military standpoint) that a war on both sides of the heavily fortified German-French border would not bring immediate victory. According to their plan (the famous-infamous Schlieffen Plan) a march through Belgium would outflank the French on their eastern border and push them in the direction of the Swiss border, and then Germany could wipe them out.

It was a scheme sure to bring England into the war, for given this scenario England had two good reasons for intervening. First, it could not stand idly by and watch the annihilation of France. A German sphere of influence that included a vanquished France and extended to the English Channel and the Atlantic Ocean would confront England with a superior continental power and pose a threat to its security. Moreover, the English and Belgian coastlines face one another. Whoever dominated the Belgian coast, especially a naval power on the order of William II's Germany, was seen as a threat to England. Antwerp had always been considered a gun pointing at the heart of England, so for geographic-strategic reasons alone the British could not tolerate an occupation of Belgium. Beyond that there was a legalistic aspect. The European powers, Germany among them, had for decades guaranteed Belgium's neutrality, and England had an enormous stake in that neutrality. It could not stand by and watch the dismantling of the Belgian buffer. The plan devised by the German General Staff simply made Bethmann's calculations an exercise in futility.

Why this problem was never discussed by the heads of the German Reich before August 1, 1914, the day the war began, is anybody's guess, for Bethmann and his predecessor, Bülow, surely must have been familiar with the Schlieffen Plan. Apparently Bethmann did not take it seriously, nor did he appreciate its political implications. It almost seems as though he assumed that military plans could be changed at will.

What then happened on August 1? The outbreak of the war was preceded by a week of hectic diplomatic activity in which England played a mediating role. London made two proposals. The first called on the ambassadors of England, Germany, France, and Italy, the four powers not directly involved in the Austro-Russian conflict, to draft a joint proposal for action by Austria and Russia. Germany rejected this because it did not want to see Austria subjected to a European tribunal. The second proposal asked Germany to persuade Austria to assure Russia that Austria was prepared to limit its war aims, perhaps by a pledge not to go beyond Belgrade, and thus stop Russia from intervening. Germany forwarded this proposal to Vienna without comment, and only later made a halfhearted attempt to press Austria on this point. In the final analysis Germany let this opportunity slip by without making any real effort. And so, on July 28, Austria declared war on Belgrade.

In response to Austria's move Russia mobilized, as did Germany. The Schlieffen Plan was implemented with the mass deployment of German troops in the West, not the East. On August 1 the German ambassador in London, where frantic negotiations were continuing, sent a cable that

Berlin misinterpreted to mean that England was willing to guarantee French neutrality if Germany remained defensive in the West and confined its troop deployment to the East. Thereupon, at a hurriedly convened meeting at the royal residence, the kaiser, in the presence of Bethmann, told Count von Moltke, the chief of the German General Staff and the nephew of the famous strategist of 1866 and 1870: "Well, we'll simply deploy all our armies in the East." This proposal met with the impassioned resistance of Moltke. He asserted that the troops already in the West could not be redeployed, lest he be left with a ragged, ill-fed, disorganized band instead of a battle-ready army in the East. The war would be lost before it got under way. The kaiser responded ungraciously: "Your uncle would have given me a different answer." That is the story as told by Moltke, who was extremely shaken, hurt, and indignant over this intervention by the kaiser.

Moltke's indignation was really misplaced. A general staff must have ready different plans for different political contingencies, and even if it prefers one particular plan, the staff must have the flexibility to substitute another one if a changed situation calls for it. Moltke had failed to do so. In 1913 he had suspended the routine planning for troop deployment in the East. In preparing for only a single eventuality the German General Staff was guilty of neglect of duty, perhaps even of criminal neglect of duty.

I mentioned earlier that Berlin had misinterpreted the cable of its ambassador in London. The British never promised to keep France neutral. They only hinted that they themselves would remain neutral for the time being if Germany would remain defensive in the West and confine its war plans to the East. Ironically, as things turned out, Germany would have been far better off militarily had it followed the British scenario. By implementing the Schlieffen Plan, Germany invited British intervention in the war on the enemy side. It thwarted Germany's political war plans and drove Bethmann to distraction. After the invasion of Belgium and the declaration of war on France, Bethmann made one last desperate attempt to dissuade the British from becoming involved in a war that was bound to tear Europe apart over a "piece of paper," as he referred to the British guarantee of Belgian neutrality. It was too late.

The kaiser's reference to the difference between Moltke and his uncle was more pertinent than he himself suspected. As long as the older Moltke was chief of staff, German military planning for a two-front war had always provided for a strategic defense in both the West and the East. Under Moltke's successor, Count von Waldersee, the strategic plans had called for a joint German-Austrian offensive in the East although the position in the West was still purely defensive. It was Schlieffen who after 1895 came up with the ambitious notion of changing a two-front war into two more-or-less successive single-front wars, to knock France out of the war before Russia could complete its mobilization, and then move against the East full force. After Schlieffen's death the younger Moltke shelved all alternative plans. This change in Germany's military strategy defines the intellectual difference between the Bismarckian and Wilhelmine eras: pessimistic caution as against an optimistic sense of power.

This sense of power was not altogether misplaced. However, it turned into a feeling of invulnerability. The Schlieffen Plan was a hubristic plan, and it failed.

Of course, all the major continental powers entered into the war with grandly conceived offensives in the hope of quick victory, and all these offensives failed: the Austrian offensive against Serbia; the Russian offensive against Austria (in Galicia) and Germany (in East Prussia); the French offensive against Germany in Lorraine and the Ardennes; and finally the German offensive against Belgium and France. In the early months of the war something became evident that, contrary to the beliefs of the various general staffs, was to shape the course of the entire war: namely, that given the state of the existing weaponry, the defensive would prove more effective than the offensive. By taking the offensive the best one could hope for was to overrun enemy terrain, but this would not knock the enemy out of the war, not even a weaker one like Serbia or Belgium. That is what made World War I into such a terrible war of attrition, a never-ending, strategically unproductive slaughter.

In this war of attrition the English blockade turned out to be a crucial weapon, if not necessarily right away, given Germany's state of preparedness. In the first year of the war Germany still had all the military supplies it needed, and the British blockade of the overseas supply routes did not yet pose any serious problems. However, there is no denying that with the passage of time Germany's economic situation, above all with regard to the food supply, deteriorated. In a war of attrition time was clearly against the Germans. Even with Austria-Hungary on its side, a blockaded Germany cut off from its overseas sources was at an economic disadvantage. Germany was starving. England and France at least had enough to eat, although the relentless German offensives took a great toll on them militarily. Were it not for the relentlessly wrong-headed strategy of its enemies, Germany could not have held out as long as it did. It would have been forced to agree to a peace, a status-quo peace, out of sheer exhaustion. Total victory may not have been in the cards for anyone in World War I, and most certainly not for Germany.

Nevertheless, Germany persisted and even drew up two new plans designed to bring victory. The first of these ultimately led to Germany's total defeat, but the second succeeded initially, and for a time it even looked as though victory was still possible. The first plan was the counterblockade of England, the U-boat war; the second involved the revolutionizing of Russia, the agreement with Lenin.

First the U-boat war: Once the war got underway, the German navy, which had played a key role in unleashing it, ceased to be much of a factor. Its ships stayed in port, with only an occasional sortie into the North Sea just to nettle the English, although one of these sorties turned into the one major sea battle of the war, the battle of Skaggerak, in which the Germans scored a tactical victory. They sank more boats than they lost, but when the smoke had cleared they had to hurry back to their home ports. Strategically nothing changed. The German fleet could not break the British blockade.

That was when the German naval command decided to call upon a still-untried, almost experimental weapon, the U-boat, to break the British blockade. They calculated that extreme ruthlessness in the deployment of the U-boats would offset their inherent weakness, and that if they sank enough British ships and created acute resupply problems, the British would be forced to get out of the war and Germany's victory would be assured. Not only did this "unlimited" U-boat war fail to live up to those high expectations, but it brought a new adversary, the hitherto neutral United States, into the war on the side of England

and France. With this, any prospect of a German victory, including the possibility of a peace through attrition, vanished. President Wilson, unlike President Roosevelt in World War II, had not intended to intervene in the war on the side of the Entente. His idea was to play the peacemaker when the time was ripe, an arbitrator with very definite ideas about the prevention of future wars. He had begun to move in that direction in 1916, but the U-boat war changed all that. Neither Wilson nor the American people were prepared to have their ships and crews sunk without warning. But as the term "unlimited" U-boat warfare implied, that precisely was the objective. It could succeed only if every ship passing through the restricted zone, including neutral ships, were sunk without warning. It was ruthless warfare, yet despite its ruthlessness the U-boat strategy of World War I was a failure. U-boats were still an impotent, untested weapon, more like submersion vessels than U-boats. They were forced to surface frequently to recharge their batteries, and on the surface they were no match for even the smallest warship. It is fair to say that even before America's entry into the war the British convoy system had rendered the U-boats ineffective.

By bringing America into the war, the unlimited U-boat offensive made Germany's position hopeless, even though there was a time lag between America's declaration of war and its active participation. In 1917 the United States did not yet have a real army nor enough tonnage for massive troop and supply shipments. Even in early 1918 American troop deployment on the Western front was comparatively light. The really massive deployment in Europe was planned for 1919. But, as we know, it never came to that.

Meanwhile, Germany came up with another design for victory—the revolutionizing of Russia. From the earliest days of the war Russia had proved to be far weaker than the German political and military leadership had calculated. This weakness can be understood only in the context of the difference in the state of industrialization of the European states. England was an established, strong industrial power; Germany had recently achieved industrial supremacy; and France had also made great strides. Only Russia was still in the early stages of industrial development. It had not begun to industrialize until the turn of the century. And even though its army was both large and brave, it was severely handicapped by its obsolete equipment. That accounts for the major defeats the Russians sustained in 1914–15, and that is why by 1917 they had reached the limits of their endurance. Moreover, Russia's size and its underdeveloped transportation system militated against the total mobilization of its limited industrial resources. By 1916 the Russian civilian population was starving; in Germany hunger did not become a factor for another year.

By and large the Russian revolution of February 1917 was a hunger protest of the cities as well as an uprising of the peasant soldiery against a devastating, unwinnable war. The Liberal Democrats who came to power in that revolution made the grave error of continuing the war despite the utter debilitation of the Russian armies. That presented Germany with the opportunity for abetting the Russian revolution by letting Lenin pass through Germany on the way to Russia.

Lenin was Germany's secret weapon in World War I. He had spent the war years in exile in Switzerland. In 1914 his party was nothing more than a marginal faction. It had always been his intention to use the war and Russia's defeat to bring about his socialist revolution in Russia, and he banked on the widespread yearning for peace to help him reach that goal. His plan jibed with Germany's hope of knocking Russia out of the war once and for all. The October Revolution of 1917 may have been Lenin's victory, but as far as the German government was concerned it was also Germany's victory—at least in the East. Lenin, however, had no intention of confining his revolution to Russia. His ultimate goal was world revolution. He hoped that the revolution in Russia would spark revolutions everywhere: in Germany and Austria and even in the West. The German government apparently was not bothered by that. They felt confident that they could vitiate this part of Lenin's strategy. Their main objective was getting Russia out of the war by encouraging internal dislocations, and in that they succeeded.

At the end of 1917 the war in the West was still bogged down and static, although America's entry threatened eventually to shift the balance to the Western powers. But now Russia was out of the war and the Germans, even though almost at the end of their tether, could wage a one-front war in the West, where they were superior, at least for the time being. For a while it seemed as though the 1914 plan for lightning victory might still be realized after all—in 1918.

The war also wrought great changes inside Germany. The first of these occurred in 1914, when the Social Democrats not only supported the war, voted for war credits, and refrained from antiwar activities—just as Bethmann had hoped and counted on—but were also beginning to exert influence in the German political machinery. The effects of the domestic revolution of 1914 cannot be overestimated. It laid the groundwork for Germany's course from 1918 to 1933.

Before 1914 the Social Democrats still were not allowed any meaningful political role. They remained the domestic enemies, the *Reichsfeind* who was not accepted as a true partner even though by 1912 the SPD had already become the strongest party in the Reichstag. The great inner-party changes that had begun prior to 1914, the gradual transition from a revolutionary to a reformist party ready to take its place alongside the other political parties, were not yet generally apparent. The war patriotism of the Social Democrats may have taken the German bourgeoisie by surprise, but it was now in full public view, and the government welcomed it.

Germany financed its war by a series of war loans, nine in all, which required confirmation by the Reichstag. This meant that upon the expiration of a loan the chancellor had to sit down and ask the parties of the Reichstag, including the Social Democrats, for their support, and in this context he of course also discussed the overall war policy. The participation of the Social Democrats in this process eventually led to a split in the party.

In 1914 the party's left wing had reluctantly acquiesced in the new patriotic orientation. By 1917 their growing disenchantment led to a split. They formed an "independent" socialist party, the USPD, which opposed the war and the war loans. This splinter group remained relatively insignificant. The majority faction continued as the strongest party in the Reichstag, and played an increasingly important role in the war and war effort. They also acted as a sort of counterweight to the grandiose military aims of the German rightists.

In the early years of the war Bethmann had managed to keep public debate about Germany's war goals to a minimum. But by 1916 debate could no longer be shut off. Two factions formed in the Reichstag: a right wing with rather extreme objectives—conquests and annexations, an expansive colonial empire, and substantial reparations—and a center-left wing which held that Germany would be lucky to get out of the war unscathed and therefore ought to grasp any opportunity for a peace and forget about annexations and reparations.

In 1917, this latter group, composed of the Social Democrats, left Liberals, and the Center, formed a new Reichstag majority. They became involved in a running public debate about war aims with the rightists—the right Liberals, the Conservatives, and the extraparliamentary Right Opposition, who now joined together to form the German Fatherland party. The debate, however, was purely academic. Before the wide-ranging goals of the rightists could become reality the war had to be won. On the other hand, a peace based on the boundaries of 1914, the goal of the new Reichstag majority, required an adversary ready to conclude such a peace, but no such willingness was to be found.

Still, or perhaps for that very reason, the debate about the war aims exacerbated the internal conflict in Germany. It was a very acrimonious debate. The one side acted as though postulating ambitious war objectives was tantamount to victory, and the other side as though a willingness to compromise automatically meant peace. Germany was a deeply divided country, although the full force of that division did not make itself felt until after the war. In point of fact, the Reichstag majority was not all that firm in its opposition to the continuing war effort and the dogged determination to hold out to the end.

In 1916–17 two major internal changes took place in Germany. In August 1916 the Second Supreme Army Command, which had already informed the chancellor in November 1914 that the war could not be won by purely military methods, was cashiered. The Supreme Command had conducted the war like an accountant: cautious deployment of manpower and matériel in the eventuality of a drawn-out war; limited military operations to keep going until the situation would allow a settlement on favorable terms. This command was dismissed in 1916 and replaced by the Third Supreme Command under Paul von Hindenburg and Erich Ludendorff, two men with close political ties to the rightists who wanted total victory, with all the potential benefits of such a victory, and who were prepared to do whatever was necessary to win this victory. The unlimited U-boat war was one of the strategies pushed through by this new command, and they also supported the revolutionizing of Russia.

The second major upheaval occurred in July 1917: the surprising cooperation of the rightist Supreme Command and the leftist Reichstag majority in the ouster of Chancellor Bethmann Hollweg. Both wanted him out, though for entirely different reasons—the Supreme Command because they did not think he was sufficiently militant, and the

Reichstag group because they did not think he was sufficiently peace-minded. Neither of them had a successor waiting in the wings. After the brief tenure of an interim appointee, the first more-or-less parliamentary chancellor—Count Hertling, an official of the Bavarian Center party—took office in December 1917. In concert with the Reichstag majority, Georg von Hertling appointed a member of the Reichstag, Friedrich von Payer, a now-forgotten leader of the Liberal party, as his vice chancellor.

In the meantime the kaiser had become completely passive. He no longer played anything like his role in the past. He vacillated between acquiescence to the Supreme Command and acquiescence to the Reichstag majority. He acted neither like the supreme commander of the armed forces nor as a knowledgeable, energetic political leader.

In 1917 the constitutional situation in Germany became muddled. At first glance nothing in the constitution appeared to have changed, but in practice it no longer worked. In the area of foreign policy the country was ruled largely by the Supreme Command, and in internal affairs by the new Reichstag majority. These two divergent, even hostile power centers cooperated on a number of issues. For example, at the end of 1916 the Supreme Command won Reichstag approval for a general mobilization (similar to the "total war" of World War II), which instituted compulsory labor service for all German males between the ages of seventeen and sixty, and potentially for women as well, and the change from industrial production to war production. The Reichstag majority voted for these measures, but at the same time it undermined them by attaching various reformist riders. The so-called Voluntary Service Law passed by the Reichstag provided for labor and management to have an equal voice in wage negotiations, and for union participation in the operation of plants. The Supreme Command reluctantly accepted these revolutionary provisions as the price for passage of its military program.

This, then, was the situation in Germany at the end of 1917: Domestically the kaiser and chancellor ceased to be in control of the country; power shifted to the Supreme Command and the Reichstag majority, respectively. By and large the two worked together, though not harmoniously. As far as the external situation was concerned, the war in the West was bogged down and the U-boat war was lost when America entered the war. On the other hand, Russia to all intents and purposes had dropped out of the picture. That being the situation at the turn of 1917–18, an exhausted, battered Reich once more, briefly, thought that victory might still be in the offing.

5

1918

Nineteen eighteen is
the turning point in the history of the German
Reich. Up to then the Reich, both structurally and
as perceived by the people, had not changed since
its founding—it was the same monarchic federation of states under Prussian hegemony with a
semiparliamentary constitution. In 1918 everything changed, and Germany has been in turmoil
ever since. The events of 1918 were contradictory,
compressed, precipitous, and to this day they have

not been completely assimilated by the German people. I shall try to shed some light on the significance of these developments.

As far as the war itself is concerned, the situation in 1918 seemed more promising than at any time since September 1914 and the collapse of the Schlieffen Plan. Nineteen eighteen was ushered in by a major peace agreement—the treaty of Brest-Litovsk between Germany and Bolshevik Russia. That got Russia out of the war in the East and freed the Germans to pursue their objective— to establish their military superiority in the West, even if it turned out to be merely temporary. Moreover, Germany had achieved almost all its objectives in the East.

In September 1914 Bethmann outlined his war aims in the East: to push Russia back from the German borders and liberate the Russian vassal states. And that is exactly what the treaty of Brest-Litovsk, an extraordinarily harsh German victorious peace, accomplished. Although a large area formerly in the possession of Russia—the Baltic states, Poland, and the Ukraine—won nominal independence, it was occupied by, and more or less dependent on, Germany. Russia had been driven back from the German borders and Germany had won from Russia a huge empire in Eastern Europe over which it could exercise direct or indirect control. Furthermore, and even more importantly, except for the requisite occupation forces in the new territories, the German eastern army was now free for deployment elsewhere.

At this point let me mention something that did not take on importance until later. In the confusion of the early days of the Russian civil war against the Bolsheviks, certain circles in the German government were eager to use the peace of Brest-Litovsk to bring all of Russia under German control. Large contingents of German troops crossed the borders established by Brest-Litovsk. In the summer of 1918 German troops occupied a line running from Narva in the north across the Dnieper River to Rostov-on-Don. That is to say, they penetrated almost as deeply as Hitler would in World War II, brought vast areas of Russia under German control, and began to toy with the idea of building a German empire on the ruins of the Bolshevik revolution. In a manner of speaking, Hitler's dream of an eastern empire already was within reach back then, as many Germans—and Hitler—knew only too well. In 1918 there was a widespread feeling that Russia could be defeated, that despite its size and vast population it was a weak country that could be vanquished and subjugated. A new idea, one not yet formulated in 1914, began to enter into German policy planning, but it did not become important until sometime later. In 1918 this notion of a German eastern empire was still nothing but a phantom vision, leaving behind only an inkling of inherent possibilities. None of this was sensed or, more accurately, known in 1918. Still the situation seemed very promising, since it was now possible to shift large numbers of crack German regiments from the East to the West. Ludendorff, the real head of the High Command under Hindenburg, had already decided on this course shortly after the Bolshevik victory in November 1917. For the first time since 1914 the prospects for military superiority in the West and for launching a successful offensive in the spring of 1918 seemed auspicious.

However, a variety of factors that should have been known to informed German circles in early 1918, when hopes for victory resurfaced once again, spoke against such a course. For one, Germany was completely exhausted. Not only the civilian population but the army as well was ill-nourished. And the situation among Germany's allies was even worse. By 1917, when Austria made a feeble effort to get out of the war, conditions there had become almost untenable. Only the hope of a German victory in 1918 persuaded Austria to remain in the alliance. The same was true of the Turks and Bulgarians. They did not want to be left out if there was a chance that the Germans might still pull it off and win the war. But all of them were ready to jump ship if things did not turn out right. If the Germans failed to score a victory in the spring and summer of 1918 they had to count on the prompt defection of their allies.

The German western offensive of 1918 was crucially important for still another reason. When America entered the war in the spring of 1917 it was not yet well prepared. Its army had to be set up and trained before it could be sent to France. With minor exceptions, American assistance was not a significant factor in 1917, but now, in 1918, the machinery was beginning to work. The first American troops arrived in France that spring, even though they still played a comparatively modest active role in the summer and fall of 1918. However, they were certain to become stronger, and by 1919 vast American armies were sure to be combat-ready. If the war in the West was not won before then it clearly could not be won at all.

The Germans thus did not have a great deal of time in which to turn things around, and if they missed this opportunity they were facing certain defeat. That was the highly dramatic situation in the beginning of 1918.

Ludendorff gambled that he would be able to penetrate the British front lines in the spring of 1918, before the Americans were ready to intervene massively. His plan for the western offensive of 1918 was not unlike a later, successful strategy: the Manstein Plan of 1940. All power was to be concentrated at the junction of the British and French forces, to break through the British front at the southern flank, and then push the isolated British troops north of the junction into the sea. Once that was done, France could be attacked head-on.

Everything hinged on the success of the first major offensive, on whether the German army would manage to penetrate all the way to the sea and drive a wedge through the British and French armies. It was a major offensive in an area that had seen much heavy fighting. In an extremely well-planned operation, three German armies were now massed against two British armies. On March 21, 1918, they attacked. From an operational standpoint, this attack was more successful than any of the Allied offensives in the West. The Germans inflicted a major defeat on one of the two British armies under attack, the southern one, regained much territory, and for a few days caused major problems for the Allies. However, the Allies were able to deal with that crisis. Once again we find that technical considerations imposed radical limits on strategy in World War I. Even as successful an offensive as this one could not guarantee a breakthrough, because the defending forces were able to bring in reinforcements and fend off the attack more rapidly than the attacker could bring in replacements.

It is important to keep in mind that World War I, the war in the West at any rate, even in this phase, was an infantry war. No army could advance more quickly than its soldiers could march. However, the defender had railroads in the rear to move in reserves from other theaters of war. That is exactly what happened here. The German offensive began on March 23, and for a few days bulletins of victorious battles, of countless prisoners, of territorial gains, poured in; then things began to slow down and finally ground to a halt. By the end of March, the German offensive had failed strategically; it got bogged down before reaching its strategic goal. It is fair to say that Germany had forfeited any chance for victory, apparent or real, in the West.

Still Ludendorff did not give up. Shortly afterward, in April, he launched a second, somewhat weaker offensive against the northern sector of the British front, and after a brief pause, still another offensive in an entirely different area, this one against the French front. In the course of this foray the Germans at the end of May and in early June once again advanced to that fateful river of 1914, the Marne. This offensive was nothing so much as an uncontrolled, desperate hitting out in all directions. It, too, scored a tactical victory, but it met with the same fate as the first one. After great initial successes it was stopped by fresh reserves without having achieved a real breakthrough. Finally a fourth offensive was launched in mid-July at Reims, which, like the Allied offensives of the previous year, was cut off before it really got underway. And with that, Germany's chances for victory in 1918 collapsed.

The reason I emphasize this point so strongly is my belief that it holds the key to the subsequent dramatic course of events of 1918. The German leadership, the German army, and to some extent the German people, insofar as they were informed, knew after mid-July that the war could not be won, that the last chance for victory had vanished. Now the Americans were coming in and making their presence felt. And once the moment of lethal danger had passed, the French and English also pulled themselves together for a great counteroffensive. It was launched on the French front on July 18, immediately following the last failed German offensive, and on August 8 on the British front, which had been reinforced by Canadian and Australian troops. August 8 is a memorable date. Ludendorff called it the "blackest day of the German army."

For the first time the Allies succeeded in something they had never managed before, something the Germans had done in the spring of 1918: win an operational victory in the initial stage of an offensive. Although they too failed to make a strategic breakthrough, it nonetheless was an unexpected and traumatic experience for the Germans. The British, Canadians, and Australians, reinforced by tanks, which for the first time played a significant role in this war, broke through the German positions, forced them into headlong retreat, and, also for the first time, took numerous prisoners.

In his memoirs, Ludendorff contends that he was told that advancing German units were greeted by shouts of "Scabs" by the retreating frontline troops. Whether or not that actually happened or is pure myth, it obviously made a profound impression on Ludendorff. He writes that the instrument with which he had waged the war, the German army, was no longer reliable: "The war had to be ended."

What had happened to the German army between March and August? In March, exhausted, ill-fed, with dwindling strength, it had once more attacked with spirit and with fleeting success, but in August it obviously was no longer ready to give its all, even defensively. During the long retreats of August and November 1918, it became clear that the morale of the German army was crumbling. Some of the troops fought as hard as ever; the imminent defeat seemed to make them even more fanatical. Heroic defensive battles were fought, but only by a segment of the troops. The morale of the others—and they were in the majority—was shattered. In effect, they had given up. What they saw was not victory but inevitable defeat, and they simply were no longer willing to risk their lives in the final chapter of a lost cause. The military naturally prefers desperate willingness to fight, but in all fairness, those who were no longer ready to give their all were neither cowards nor deserters, but the thoughtful members of the army. The mass armies of World War I were

thinking armies, unlike the old professional armies, which were machines, drilled in order and obedience. There was a saying that thinking should
be left to horses because they had bigger heads.
Toward the end of the war the army leadership
could no longer count on the blind obedience of
the old standing army. This new army was made
up of thinking citizens. In order to fight at top
efficiency they needed not only military discipline
but also what nowadays is called motivation. They
had to feel that they were fighting for something
worthwhile. I am not talking of ideals but simply
of the chance of victory.

Objectively speaking, this possibility no
longer existed after July, or perhaps even after
April 1918. The Germans had shot the last arrow
in their quiver and failed to hit the target. After
that they fought to postpone the inevitable. The
idea of sacrifice without the prospect of victory is
bound to produce psychological and physical
exhaustion.

Ludendorff was absolutely right when he said
that the collapse of the fighting spirit took place
in the army itself, not among the civilians in the
hinterland, who, misled by unduly optimistic
army bulletins, still clung to a blind belief in the
possibility of victory. It was the army that, in the
spring and summer of 1918, suffered a setback that
does not show up on any war maps because it was
a matter of morale. The enthusiastic German
army of 1914 was no more. Even if some of the

troops continued to fight with fervor, the morale of the army on the whole was, if not completely shattered, badly impaired. Ludendorff was unquestionably right in August 1918 when he concluded that the war had to be ended.

But how? In the meantime the Western powers had become convinced that they had crossed the critical barrier and that they could risk an offensive without waiting for the Americans. To their surprise, they discovered that their counterattack was successful. After August the German army, still fighting, though not with its customary zeal, continued to fall back from one position to the other. By the end of September they had reached the so-called Hindenburg Line, the last defensive line far behind the old front, and that is where the Allies, after a brief pause, unleashed the full force of their counteroffensive. Now the Allies were threatening to break through the Hindenburg Line, and that meant the collapse of the western front.

In this situation Ludendorff decided to throw in the towel. On September 28 he and Hindenburg agreed to ask for a cease-fire based on President Wilson's Fourteen Points. If Hindenburg and Ludendorff had really read the Fourteen Points they would have known that they were predicated on the unconditional defeat of Germany. They called not only for the return of Alsace-Lorraine to France, but also for the restoration of Poland, including the Prussian-Polish area and Poland's access to the sea—that is, the future Polish Corridor. I doubt that Ludendorff had really studied the Fourteen Points closely. He just tossed them into the ring to make it difficult for the Americans to reject Germany's cease-fire and peace offer.

The next day, Sunday, September 29, something else happened that was bound to have crucial consequences. Ludendorff had asked two senior members of the civilian government, Chancellor Count Hertling and Foreign Minister Paul von Hintze, to meet with him at his headquarters. They arrived separately. Hintze, the younger of the two, traveled overnight and met with Ludendorff that Sunday morning; Hertling traveled by day and did not arrive at headquarters until late in the afternoon. Hintze took advantage of Hertling's absence to present Ludendorff with a new plan. He thought that the cease-fire would stand a better chance of acceptance by Wilson if a parliamentary-democratic government were formed in Germany to persuade the Americans that it was a new, democratic Germany that was suing for peace—and moreover a peace based on Wilson's own peace program. This meant that they would have to ask the Reichstag majority to form a government and to revise the constitution, making the Reich a constitutional monarchy in which the Reichstag would have the power to depose the government by a vote of no confidence. Moreover, it was necessary to create the impression that Germany was seeking peace not because of the threat of military collapse but because of this democratic reorganization.

Ludendorff liked Hintze's plan, not least because he probably had his own agenda as well. I am convinced that he understood the psychological-diplomatic considerations underlying Hintze's proposal, but beyond that he also realized that if he went along with Hintze's plan he would be spared the onus of personally raising the white flag. He could put the burden on the shoulders of his domestic foes, the Reichstag majority.

Thus on September 29, in the presence of the kaiser—who had remained passive through all of this—the headquarters meeting decided to form a parliamentary government composed of ministers of the Reichstag majority and to instruct this government to seek an immediate cease-fire. The Supreme Command was not to play any official role in this, for according to Ludendorff the collapse of the western front appeared to be imminent. In return for its help, the new government was to be allowed to revise the constitution and to transform the Reich into a parliamentary government.

On October 2, the leaders of the Reichstag in Berlin learned about this plan from an emissary of Ludendorff. They were bewildered. The news that the war in the West was lost and that the collapse of the military was imminent came as a shock to all of them, including the members of the Reichstag majority. And linked to this shocking news was the request that they take over the bankrupt store, announce the bankruptcy, and accept responsibility for something they had had no hand in.

In these dark hours it was the Social Democrats who jumped into the breach. They had been preparing for such an unlikely turn of events since before the war. Their decision was to prove crucial in the coming weeks and months. The Social Democrats, the majority wing at any rate, were ready to assume greater responsibility than any of the other parties. If we are now given responsibility, said their chairman, Friedrich Ebert, we have no choice but to jump in and salvage what can still be salvaged, particularly if we are asked to negotiate the cease-fire and are also granted something we have been advocating for decades: a parliamentary government and the power to dismiss the government by a vote of no confidence, and beyond that the abolition of the Prussian three-tier suffrage. These were the last important demands still open on the Social Democratic agenda. Now these demands were being met. Led by Ebert, the Social Democrats after some debate accepted the offer.

The significance of this move cannot be overestimated. Bismarck's enemies of the state, the outsiders, the still ostracized "unpatriotic band" of William II, were about to become the governing party of the Reich and of the empire (at the time there was still no talk of abdication); they even stood ready to shoulder responsibility for the defeat. It was an epic turn of events.

Prince Max von Baden, a liberal aristocrat and member of the ruling Badense family, formed a government composed of Social Democrats, left Liberals, and Centrists. On October 3 this government, without reference to either the military situation or the role of the Supreme Command, submitted a cease-fire and peace offer to President Wilson. The emperor himself persuaded a reluctant Prince Max to do so.

The military collapse of the western front, which Ludendorff had expected on September 28 and 29, did not occur. The German army, even though in helpless retreat, continued to fight up to the day of the armistice, November 11. In those final days of the war, 250,000 Germans were taken prisoner. A cohesive force continued to fight on Belgian and French soil to the very last day of the war. But on the other hand, now, and only now, the home front began to crumble. The mass of Germans, particularly the starving, dissatisfied workers, the traditional backbone of the leftist parties, suddenly, in the face of all those proclaimed victories, were told that the war was lost, or at least was presumed to be lost. No wonder the people lost all confidence in the leaders who had brought them to this pass. A revolution was brewing in Germany's cities. True, it was only brewing, it had not yet erupted; but the domestic political landscape in Germany was changing radically in October 1918.

And something else was happening that October. Wilson did not immediately accept Germany's proffered cease-fire. He sent a note in which, not entirely without reason, he questioned the genuineness of Germany's sudden democratization (the emperor and the princes were after all still in place), and in a series of notes he demanded further changes: true democratization and the removal of the kaiser.

With Wilson's demands on the table, a debate about the future of the monarchy began in Germany. The question was whether, since no turning back was possible, Wilson's demands should be met: whether the kaiser should be forced to abdicate. A new government party was formed, one that advocated sacrificing the emperor as a figurehead, even if not the monarchy itself. Others, particularly circles with links to the army and navy, were opposed to this.

Ludendorff underwent a strange transformation in October. He had staged his coup—for that is what his September 29 meeting amounted to—while in a state of panic over the imminent collapse of the western front. But when that collapse did not occur, and the western front continued to fight, Ludendorff once again changed his mind and decided to hold out and fight to the last. From a purely military perspective it might perhaps have been possible to hold out in the West until the winter. Even though the Allied offensives continued to press on, no real breakthrough was being made. And now it was October. By winter, operations would probably have to be halted; on the western front the Antwerp-Maas Line might perhaps be consolidated once more for a new spring and summer offensive. However, given the expected massive American power, the situation appeared utterly hopeless and would most likely have resulted in the occupation of Germany.

However, what happened now made any further resistance in the West illusory. The Central Powers collapsed. Actually they had already come to the end of the rope earlier that year, and had only held on in the hope of one last big German offensive, a final German triumph. When that did not come to pass, Austria, Bulgaria, and Turkey disintegrated. In Austria the nationalities began to stir. The Austrian army became almost irrelevant. The first front to fall apart was the Austro-Bulgarian Balkan front, followed by Austria's collapse in Italy. Even if the Germans had been able to hold the western front through the winter, a new southern front now threatened to open up, and there Germany stood defenseless.

These were the complex conditions under which German domestic policy now had to be conducted. As I mentioned earlier, by the end of October the old adversarial divisions resurfaced in Germany: on the one side were the proponents of one final desperate stand; on the other, the proponents of an end to the war whatever the cost. In early November this conflict culminated in a revolution no one could have predicted.

The German revolution was sparked by a decision of the Naval High Command—reached without either the knowledge or concurrence of the government—to launch a major assault on the British fleet. A portion of the German fleet refused to carry out the orders for this engagement, and in the end the plan had to be scuttled. The mutinying sailors were arrested and threatened with court-martial and execution. This brought many who had not joined in the mutiny over to the side of their jailed comrades, and on November 4 the sailors at the Kiel naval base, the home port of the western fleet, revolted. They took over the ships, hoisted the red flag, formed sailors' councils, and took over the city of Kiel.

This revolt, which coincided with the debate over the fate of the emperor, had no clearly articulated political goals. But once the sailors took over the fleet and the city of Kiel, they realized that they had to see things through if they wished to avoid court-martial and execution. They fanned out from Kiel and within a week, beginning on November 4, the revolution spread like wildfire across northern Germany, then westward, and ultimately through most of Germany. In addition, there were spontaneous uprisings in a number of German cities, among them the November 7 revolution in Munich.

It was a leaderless yet unstoppable process, a spontaneous mass movement. Soldiers' councils formed in the home army, and workers' councils in the plants. These workers' and soldiers' councils played a sort of administrative role in the big cities. The October government was not all that firmly established, and it did not welcome the revolution.

In his memoirs Prince Max von Baden tells of a meeting he had with Ebert on November 7:

> I met with Ebert in the early morning in the garden. I told him of my planned trip: "You know what I have in mind. If I manage to persuade the emperor to step down will you then support me in my fight against the social revolution?" Ebert answered promptly and unambiguously: "If the emperor does not abdicate, the social revolution is inevitable. But I do not want it. Yes, I hate it like sin."

That was Ebert's subjective truth. In October he and his party had reached all their domestic goals. Now they wanted to put an end to the war as quickly as possible and, together with the progressive and centrist parties of the Reich, continue to govern as regents, as a kind of constitutional monarchy. Therefore a revolution was the very last thing they wanted at this point. But the revolution was apparently unstoppable. On Saturday, November 9, it spread to Berlin. A general strike was called. The workers took to the streets and marched to the Reichstag without making any specific demands other than the end of the war. But Philip Scheidemann, the co-leader of the Social Democrats, thought he had to offer them something more, and stepping out on the balcony to address the crowd he proclaimed the German republic. That was not what Ebert had had in mind, and the two had a public argument in the Reichstag restaurant. Ebert said that whatever the future shape of the German Reich, whether monarchy or republic, the decision was not theirs to make but was up to a constituent assembly.

Ebert for his part was willing to preserve the monarchy. That is why, that same afternoon—an intriguing footnote to German history—he tried to reverse Scheidemann's proclamation. He received Prince Max von Baden, who in the interim had announced the emperor's abdication and in violation of the constitution had handed over the chancellorship to Ebert. Ebert asked Prince Max in his capacity of regent to keep open the possibility of saving the monarchy. But the prince declined. He had had enough. He wanted to return to private life. Ebert was forced to accept the German republic as a fait accompli.

The republic became reality not only because of Scheidemann's proclamation. A great deal else was going on. The emperor had not actually abdicated, although he had fled to Holland the night of November 9. However, almost all the other German nobles, the kings of Bavaria, Saxony, and Württemberg, and the archdukes and dukes of the other German states, did abdicate in early November, some sooner than others. It was strange, since none of them had been physically threatened. Delegates of the workers' and soldiers' councils had simply gone to them and asked them to abdicate, and they complied without resistance.

Amidst the confusion of those November days this silent disappearance of all German monarchies, those hitherto esteemed, unopposed, unquestioned institutions, went *almost* unnoted. Strangely enough, it has also been practically ignored by German historiography; no convincing explanation has been offered. Some of those who abdicated seemed almost relieved. Thus the king of Saxony told the delegation that came to ask him to step down: "Well, all right, you can take care of the mess yourselves," an apt summing up of the whole affair.

The German monarchs no longer wanted to govern. They wanted to return to their generally very comfortable private lives. Unlike their French and British counterparts in their respective revolutions, not a single one was arrested, let alone executed. The German revolution, if it can be called that, was easygoing. Still, it was like an earthquake that could not be checked.

To get back to the emperor: On October 29 he had gone to the headquarters in Spa. At first he was quite willing to accept the parliamentary reforms and to continue to rule as a constitutional monarch. He ignored the plea of a Prussian minister who came to see him at Spa and asked him to abdicate. The revolution took him by surprise, yet he still hoped to put it down with the help of the returning army. But the events of November 9 put an end to that hope.

The failure of the major German offensive affected the morale of the German army. Nor did the offer of a cease-fire and Germany's internal upheavals improve matters. On November 9 the Supreme Command ordered thirty-nine frontline commanders, mostly divisional officers, to headquarters to find out whether the army, in the event of a cease-fire, would be willing to fight for the monarchy, for the emperor, against the revolution. The unanimous response of the assembled officers was a resounding no. The army, they said, was prepared to escort His Majesty back to Germany if he so desired, but the men did not want to continue fighting, either outside or inside the country.

Thereupon Hindenburg and Ludendorff's successor, General Wilhelm Groener, decided to advise the emperor to abdicate, or at least to go into exile. On November 9 the emperor acceded to their advice—again, oddly enough, without resistance. He sought exile in Holland, and with that put an end not only to his personal reign but, as it turned out, to any chance for a future restoration of the monarchy. His formal abdication, which came only later that month, was practically meaningless.

Two decisions put an end to the German monarchy on November 9: the emperor's flight to Holland and Prince Max von Baden's refusal to accept the regency and preserve the German monarchy, though not necessarily a Hohenzollern monarchy. Ebert as the new chancellor and head of government was left to deal with the revolution and the task of negotiating the cease-fire.

The cease-fire was a controversial issue in the Allied camp as well. The American commander in Europe, General Pershing, did not want it. The Germans had been defeated, he said, so why grant them a cease-fire that would allow them to dig in behind the Rhine and continue fighting? Like President Roosevelt in World War II, Pershing wanted unconditional surrender.

The French and British high commands were more receptive to the idea of a cease-fire. Their armies, like those of the Germans, had been bled white. Unlike the Americans, they were not interested in any major future offensives. It was finally agreed to accept the German offer of a truce under conditions that would preclude any resumption of hostilities.

On November 6, the Germans were asked to send a delegation to Allied headquarters to receive the conditions for a cease-fire. Mathias Erzberger, a Center party deputy and a minister in the cabinet of Max von Baden, headed the delegation. It is worth noting that the man chosen to sign a military truce was not a general but a civilian government official.

The conditions of the cease-fire were extremely harsh. They sealed the defeat of the Reich and ruled out any further resistance. The Allies demanded the prompt evacuation of the still occupied territories and of all German territories on the left bank of the Rhine as well as of three bridgeheads. The Allied armies were to follow in the footsteps of the departing German troops and occupy the territories on the left bank and the three bridgeheads on the right bank. In addition, the German fleet and vast quantities of matériel were to be handed over to the victors. Those were the principal conditions. They made it unmistakably clear to the Germans that they had lost the war, and put the stamp on Germany's defeat, for they ruled out any possibility of future resistance beyond the Rhine.

On November 6, while the revolution was spreading throughout Germany, Erzberger went to Compiègne to meet with Marshal Foch, was handed the conditions for the cease-fire, negotiated about some details, and submitted them to his government, which in turn submitted them to the Supreme Command. The Supreme Command stated that they had no choice but to accept them even if no further concessions were forthcoming, since they were in no position to continue the war.

Erzberger signed. The armistice took effect on November 11.

How did the German people react to this? Until August they had been led to believe that Germany was winning. Only in October, when a cease-fire was first mentioned, did they learn that the government—though not necessarily the Supreme Command—considered the situation hopeless. Then, on November 9, the Social Democrats became the ruling party, there was a revolution, and the princes abdicated; presumably the emperor abdicated as well. At any rate, he fled.

What did all this mean? The mass of not particularly well-informed Germans saw the situation thus: Just as we were about to win the war those characters who always wanted a negotiated peace took over the government and threw in the towel. Then came the revolution and they signed an armistice that made us powerless.

That was the basis for the later "stab-in-the-back" myth, first openly proclaimed by Ludendorff, although Ebert of all people had already paved the way for it. Ebert's main domestic concern was to salvage whatever could still be salvaged: to carry on either with a constitutional monarchy, or with a republic if need be, and to suppress the revolution. To begin with, Ebert concluded a pseudo-armistice with the revolution. On November 10, at a meeting of the Berlin workers' and soldiers' councils, he got himself appointed as head of a six-man Council of People's Delegates, and for the second time became head of the government. But in fact he made a pact with remnants of the Supreme Command, or rather with its de facto chief, General Groener.

That same evening the two had a critical, by now famous, telephone conversation. Ebert, even though not the legitimate chancellor (although he had dual legitimacy—through appointment by Prince Max von Baden and through his post with the revolutionary Berlin workers' and soldiers' councils) tried to resurrect the October agreement with the Supreme Command. He wanted to use the returning army units to suppress the revolution in the hope of winning the support of the Supreme Command for the new government and the new constitution. Groener agreed, and to underscore his support he staged a counterrevolution in which he used the army to suppress the left revolution led by the Council of People's Delegates (headed, ironically, by Ebert himself).

In the so-called stab-in-the-back trial of 1925, Groener under oath told of his conversation with Ebert:

> To begin with the issue was—and that was my thinking and the immediate goal—to take power away from the workers' and soldiers' councils in Berlin. With that in mind an undertaking was planned involving the military entry of ten divisions into Berlin. An officer was dispatched to Berlin to discuss the

details also with the Prussian minister of war, who naturally could not be left out. There were some problems. As I recall, the independent members of the government, the so-called people's delegates, but I think also the soldiers' councils—I cannot give the details offhand—demanded that the troops move in without live ammunition. We of course opposed this, and Mr. Ebert naturally promptly agreed that the troops come to Berlin with live ammunition.

We worked out a plan for the troops moving into Berlin. One of their tasks was to help establish a stable government. This plan had a day-by-day schedule: the disarming of Berlin, the cleaning out of the Spartacists from Berlin, etc. All that was provided for, a day-by-day plan for the individual divisions. That was also discussed with Mr. Ebert by the officer I had sent to Berlin. I am particularly grateful to Mr. Ebert for that and for his unswerving love of country and complete dedication to the cause, and have defended him against all who attacked him. Our plan was drawn up in cooperation with and with the concurrence of Mr. Ebert.

The detailed Ebert-Groener agreement coincided with the army's withdrawal from the occupied areas and return home. Ebert greeted the returning soldiers in Berlin in early December with words that anticipated the stab-in-the-back legend: "You were not beaten by any enemy. Only when the opponent's superiority of men and matériel became more pressing did *we* give up the fight. . . . *You* can return with head held high."

To begin with, the Ebert-Groener agreement failed. On December 16 an All-German Workers' and Soldiers' Council congress was scheduled to be held in Berlin. The plan was for the returning ten divisions to stage a countercoup to prevent this meeting. According to Groener's sworn testimony, the soldiers could no longer be counted on. This was not the old German army of the four war years. Once they got to Berlin, the soldiers dispersed and went home; their units practically dissolved. When the All-German congress met on December 16, the ten divisions had dwindled to a total of eight hundred men. Ever since the summer, a silent revolution in morale had been underway, a very different revolution than the one that later swept the country, though of course they were not entirely unrelated. The army at any rate could no longer be counted on in a domestic political power struggle.

Consequently, the Supreme Command meeting at Kassel decided to remove all obstacles to the demobilization of the army and instead to recruit a volunteer force, the Free Corps, made up of soldiers who had not taken part in the army's internal revolution, who had continued to fight fanatically to the very end, who opposed what was happening at home, who were loyal to the emperor and to Ludendorff, and who stood ready to reverse the events of November by force. The Ebert government, and particularly the new minister of defense, Gustav Noske, now entered into an agreement with this volunteer army.

The year 1918 ended with the first pitched street battles in Berlin, in which the revolutionary People's Naval Division defeated the remnants of the old army. The new year began with the so-called Spartacus Week in Berlin, in which the first Free Corps brutally put down a new revolutionary upsurge.

We have now come to the end of 1918. I would like to add that what happened in Berlin in December and January was not limited to that city. Similar events were taking place throughout Germany in the first half of 1919. It was a sort of insidious civil war in which the Free Corps, with the full protection of the Ebert-Noske government and later, after Ebert became president, of the Scheidemann-Noske government, brutally put down the last remnants of the workers' and soldiers' councils in numerous German cities. The Reichstag majority led by the Social Democrats in union with the counterrevolutionary forces of the old army effectively nullified the revolution of November 1918. Only one result of that revolution remained unchanged: the end of the monarchy.

Let me mention yet another point. The mood of the German people mirrored the events of 1918.

Among those affected by these events was a failed artist, an Austrian who had been a volunteer in the German army. He had been gassed and was hospitalized in Pomerania when news of the end of the war reached him. It was there that he decided to become politically active to undo all those terrible things he thought had been allowed to happen in 1918—the seeming loss of nerve of the homefront, the seeming failure to grasp a victory apparently within reach. The name of that man whom no one knew was Adolf Hitler, and in the next ten years he gradually evolved into a key figure of German political life.

6

Weimar and Versailles

THE NATIONAL ASSEMBLY elected in January 1919 met in Weimar rather than in turbulent Berlin, partly because of Weimar's quiet charm and sheltered setting and partly because its intellectual tradition appealed to the new Germany.

The adoption of the new constitution was neither the most important nor the most vexing problem facing the Weimar National Assembly. Rather, it was the final draft of the Versailles

Treaty submitted to Germany in April 1919. When the contents of the draft treaty were made public in May 1919, all Germans, ordinary citizens as well as the National Assembly and the government, were thunderstruck. In addition to almost complete disarmament, huge reparations, and the forfeiture of its colonies, Germany was asked to relinquish territories east, west, and north—demands everyone felt to be monstrous. The Versailles Agreement did not treat Germany like an enemy who, though vanquished, was still a member of the community of nations, but rather like a prisoner awaiting his sentence. The initial general reaction was, "Don't sign."

What would have happened had Germany refused to sign? It is safe to assume that the Allies would have resumed hostilities, pushed on into Germany, where they would have encountered little or no military resistance, and occupied Germany up to the Weser River. Under the pressure of the military ultimatum, and after a great deal of in-fighting and the reorganization of the government, the Versailles Treaty was signed.

The government and the majority of the National Assembly feared that an Allied occupation would mean the end of the Reich. It was assumed that, in that event, the Allies would make separate agreements with the south German states and with some newly formed states in northern Prussia. With that, the Reich would be split into two: a western region occupied by the Western powers, and the old Prussia and Saxony in the east and northeast. In retrospect, knowing what we do about post–World War II Germany, we must ask ourselves whether that really would have been all that terrible. The end result would have been the same as what ultimately happened after World War II: a German western state that sooner or later would have been compelled to ally itself with the Western powers, and a German eastern state—and moreover an entity still in possession of the eastern Prussian provinces—whose ultimate fate cannot be guessed, for it was and is difficult to conjecture about an Allied occupation beyond the Weser.

Would the governments of southern Germany and those that would have arisen in northwestern Germany eventually have signed? And in case a German government continued to function in Berlin, would the Allies not have had to occupy eastern Germany as well? And would a Germany occupied by the Western powers, similar to the post-1945 structure, but without the Russians and without the loss of the eastern provinces, not have been preferable to the outcome of World War II? And since the Allies eventually would have been forced to install a German government, the occupation most likely would not have lasted forever.

Those are open questions. If the Germans had refused to sign the Versailles Treaty they might possibly have had the same chance of preserving the Reich as by signing. But even by signing, the Germans in the long run had a much greater political opportunity than they realized at the time. For, looked at dispassionately, the Paris Treaty, of which Versailles was only a part, the part that directly concerned Germany, did not really have any adverse effects on Germany's potential major-power status. True, the disarmament provisions and reparations were extremely onerous. But as for the rest, the position of Germany in Europe, a Germany still intact despite territorial losses in the west, east, and north, was by no means weaker than prior to 1914. On the contrary.

Before 1914 the German Reich was, in a then popular word, "encircled"—surrounded by the four great powers—England, France, Austria-Hungary, and Russia. Three of these, England, France, and Russia, were allied against Germany in World War I. Later, one of those major powers, Austria-Hungary, fell apart and was replaced by weak successor states which, because of their size alone, could never hope to gain major-power status. Sooner or later they would have had to come under the influence of the nearest bigger power—that is, Germany. Russia, now the Soviet Union, lay outside the European system of states. Like Germany it was, to put it bluntly, ostracized. And so Russia began to send out feelers, not to the West but to its fellow outcast, Germany.

Consequently, after the war Germany's position was stronger than before, because so much in the adjacent areas had changed in Germany's favor. The results of the war, and the peace treaty itself, solidified Germany's positional advantage, except in the event of another war, while the disadvantageous features, disarmament and reparations, were temporary. Only ten years after the war nobody was prepared to fight another war to prevent Germany from rearming or to force it to pay reparations. This meant that in the long run the results of War War I strengthened rather than weakened Germany's position.

The Western powers for their part were anything but unified. They had reached agreement on the peace treaties only after a great deal of bickering. And then the strongest member of that alliance dropped out. The United States did not ratify the Versailles agreement, pulled back from European affairs, and refused to honor a promised guarantee for French claims. That meant that the Versailles agreement was supported by only two powers, England and France.

Their victory over Germany had not been easy, and it seemed unlikely that they would be able to keep Germany down permanently. Moreover, before long, disagreement broke out between them.

England was satisfied with the Versailles Treaty. The German fleet had already been handed over to England in the cease-fire, and Versailles barred Germany from building up its navy. Germany had lost its colonies, which were given to the British dominions and in part to England itself. England had achieved its war aims. France, on the other hand, had not. After a draining, devastating war, France, with its population of forty million, still faced a seventy-million-strong, undivided, cohesive Germany, a Germany that, once it recovered and threw off the burdens of Versailles, might again become superior. Consequently, France like Germany became a revisionist power after 1919. The Versailles Treaty did not satisfy France's needs, and self-interest dictated that it try to revise it at Germany's expense. Germany for its part was also determined to get the agreement revised, above all to get rid of those two nagging burdens—disarmament and reparations— twin obstacles in the path of a stronger Germany.

Although there was unanimous agreement in Germany that the treaty was unacceptable, that it had to be revised, there was no agreement over what should be stricken first. Was it more important to try and circumvent the disarmament clauses and to reassert a military presence or should the scuttling of reparations take priority, to reestablish Germany's position in the world by rebuilding the German economy?

The first approach was the preference of the Reichswehr, the Germany army, and in particular of its then commander in chief, General Hans von Seeckt. Initially his view prevailed. Seeckt made it clear that he could reach his goal only by working with Russia. And so, beginning in the twenties, the Reichswehr and the Red Army began their secret cooperation. The Soviet Union provided the Reichswehr with terrain for military exercises, with arms, tanks, airplanes, and chemical weapons barred by the Versailles Treaty. In return, the Reichswehr helped the new Red Army train its soldiers, and advised it on strategy. A German military consultant in the Soviet Union, General Köstring, reported in 1935, after an outstanding Soviet performance: "We can take satisfaction in this. After all, their commanders are our pupils."

Still another opportunity for military cooperation with Soviet Russia soon presented itself. In 1920, after Poland attacked Russia, war broke out between the two countries. Russia was expected to win. The Russians got as far as Warsaw. Even back then Seeckt already thought that in case of a Russian victory Germany ought to attack Poland and divide the spoils with Russia and at least regain what had been lost in 1919 at Versailles.

However, Poland won, so that plan fizzled. The Russians did not annex any Polish territories. On the contrary, Poland annexed large parts of Byelorussia and the Ukraine. That is how matters would stand until 1939. But this outcome also favored Germany. It exacerbated the hostility between Poland and Russia, and this in turn helped the Seeckt wing of the Reichswehr to work toward a German-Russian alliance and a German-Russian war against Poland. The Reichswehr even managed to win the temporary support of the German foreign-policy establishment, which generally pursued a different course. That temporary alliance produced the first sensational postwar agreement, the Rapallo Treaty of 1922 between Germany and the Soviet Union. It exploded like a bombshell in the midst of an international economic conference in Genoa and gave rise to profound and lasting misgivings over Germany's motives, to the so-called Rapallo Complex.

Looked at superficially, the Rapallo Treaty was an innocuous document, an overdue accord between Germany and the Soviet Union. Since Versailles had nullified the treaty of Brest-Litovsk, the new Germany decided to enter into official diplomatic relations with the new Russia—the Western powers had not yet done so—to draw up trade agreements with reciprocal most-favored-nation clauses, and on the whole to resume normal relations. In itself there was nothing objectionable about any of this. But of course there was more to this treaty than meets the eye.

After Rapallo the unofficial German-Russian military cooperation became more formal, and it lasted until 1933. The possibility of a joint campaign against Poland was not abandoned by either of the two military commands. The cooperation between Germany and Russia may be said to have brought the Reichswehr closer to its primary objective: the circumvention of the military provisions of the Versailles Treaty.

The priorities of the German Foreign Office

and the government, however, were of an altogether different order. Their primary goal was to shed the reparations burden. That is why German policymakers were willing to chart the catastrophic course that destroyed the country's social fabric, the devastating, galloping inflation that began in 1919 and reached its climax in 1923.

Even before the bizarre situation of 1923, all German monetary wealth had already been destroyed between 1919 and 1922. At the end of the war, the ratio of the German mark to the dollar was 1 to 10, but by 1922 it was 1 to 20,000. In other words, Germany's monetary assets had disappeared. A sweeping redistribution of wealth from thrifty savers to property owners was underway, though this too had some transitory economic advantages.

From 1919 to 1923 Germany had full employment, even though real wages declined. At the expense of those who had been thrifty and saved their money, German industry was able to avoid the mass unemployment that other countries experienced after demobilization. Germany's exports rose at an unprecedented rate, albeit at constantly falling prices, and plants kept producing. Thus the first victims of the inflation were not the workers but the thrifty burgers. They were in effect expropriated, and that of course created enormous bitterness. Stefan Zweig wrote that nothing made the German middle class so receptive to Hitler's message as the inflation of

1919–22. Their bitterness was not completely unfounded. Not only did the government watch inflation go into orbit, but it used it for its own purposes. If Germany no longer possessed an internationally accepted currency with which to pay its debt, they reasoned, then Germany might perhaps be able to shake off the burdensome reparations.

The reparations issue served the interests of both German and French revisionism. The Germans let inflation run on to avoid paying reparations. The French tried to use Germany's failure to meet its obligations to revise the territorial stipulations of the Versailles Treaty. In 1923, the revisionist efforts of the two adversaries culminated in the Ruhr conflict.

Prior to the Ruhr affair, France had taken action against Germany in retaliation for Germany's failure to meet its monetary obligations. France would make occasional forays across the Rhine and occupy cities on the right bank. Then in 1923 France decided on a major move—to occupy the Ruhr valley, Germany's most important industrial region and prime economic asset. France used military force to pry the Ruhr loose from Germany economically and, later, politically as well.

Germany responded by passive resistance. Production in the Ruhr ground to a halt. And since the population, workers and employers alike, had to be kept alive, the Treasury's printing presses came to the rescue, printing paper money by the bushel. The presses could not keep pace with the demand. By 1923 the production of all that paper money posed a real problem. Private printing presses had to pitch in. The mass of paper created transportation problems. Entire freight trains were comandeered to help ship these piles of banknotes.

By 1923 the passive resistance in the Ruhr and the methods used to finance it had brought Germany's "money" economy to a virtual standstill. Everyone in Germany was familiar with the daily fluctuation of the dollar-mark exchange rate. It was like a fever chart. In the beginning of 1923 a dollar cost twenty thousand marks. By August it had climbed to a million, and three months later to a billion. At the end of 1923 a dollar cost 4.2 trillion marks. To all intents and purposes Germany no longer had a currency.

Before 1923 the inflation had wiped out only monetary *wealth*, but now monetary *income* also lost its value. Workers and the thrifty middle class alike had become the victims of inflation. In effect, work was no longer compensated in money, or only in money that lost its value within the hour. It was an absurd situation, and in the fall of 1923 it led to a political crisis. At stake was Germany's political survival. Regardless of its positive value, the passive resistance in the Ruhr obviously had to be stopped. Germany's other creditors, England and the United States, had become convinced that things could not go on this way. They put pressure on France to end the Ruhr adventure. And Germany finally had to do something that should have been done in 1919–20: revalue the currency.

The new stable currency made it possible for Germany to renegotiate the terms of the reparations agreement. Under the new terms Germany was to pay moderate annual installments of two billion marks on a yet-to-be-determined total amount. As security Germany had to pledge some of its revenues, primarily customs and railway revenues. Beyond that, the western borders were to be firmly fixed in an agreement between Germany, England, the United States, and France, in order to forestall future border violations by France and territorial revisions by Germany.

The upshot of all this was a new peace agreement in 1924–25. It consisted of two parts: the London Agreement of 1924 on the reparations question, and the Locarno Treaty of 1925, in which Germany unconditionally and voluntarily renounced all claims on Alsace-Lorraine and agreed to demilitarize the occupied left bank of the Rhine once the occupation ended. In exchange Germany won an extremely valuable concession, a British-Italian guarantee of the newly agreed-upon German-French western border.

Locarno meant that France in effect broke away from its East European alliance. If the German western border was guaranteed by Italy and England, then France would not be permitted to cross it if Germany were to get involved in a war with the Poles or the Czechs, France's allies in the

East. The conclusion France drew from this implicit result of Locarno was to switch to a purely defensive strategy. In the wake of Locarno, France built the Maginot Line and proclaimed to all the world that it no longer considered itself a leading European power and the guarantor of the new Central and East European national states. Its sole concern was with its own security and a desire to learn to live with Germany.

France had tried to avert such a course by pushing for an Eastern Locarno, that is, a guarantee of Germany's eastern border, particularly the Polish-German border, by England, Italy, and France itself. However, this was roundly rejected not only by Germany but by England and Italy as well. And for good reason. It was not at all certain that the Western powers would be able to guarantee Poland's borders in the event of a German war in the East. As we found out in World War II, these doubts were well founded. An Eastern Locarno would have required Soviet agreement, but the Soviet Union was not part of the European power structure. Moreover, the Soviet Union had no intention of guaranteeing any of Poland's borders against Germany, particularly in view of its own territorial designs on Poland.

The situation after Locarno thus looked like this: The Germans were quietly but effectively working with the Soviet Union in the East to undermine the military provisions of the Versailles Treaty. In the West they had something like a new peace with France, England, and Italy, an appendix to the Versailles Treaty designed to forestall a war between France and Germany. For the time being the Reich had to continue to pay reparations, moderate annual installments on an unspecified total sum. Furthermore, the United States had become involved in the European economy in a way that promised to be of greater help to Germany than to the others.

True, France and England were Germany's creditors, but they were also indebted to the United States. The war had been financed largely by the United States, and the Americans insisted on the repayment of these war loans. France and England paid, even if reluctantly. A sort of circular economic process was underway: Germany paid reparations to England and France, who in turn paid war debts to America, who, in order to keep it all moving along, pumped loans into Germany. The years 1924 to 1929 became a period of rebuilding in Germany, even of a mild prosperity, only because America's loans exceeded Germany's reparations payments. It has been established that in these years Germany paid out roughly ten billion marks in reparations and received about twenty-five billion in American credits. And its revitalized economy enabled Germany to become an exporter.

The man who presided over all these agreements and revisions of Versailles was Gustav Stresemann, Germany's foreign minister, although he never expressed satisfaction over what he had won. He rarely discussed his revisionist goals, but at various times he hinted at them, so it is possible to guess what he had in mind.

His immediate goal was the evacuation of the left bank of the Rhine by the British and French occupation forces. He won that, although he did not live to see it. The evacuation, agreed to in 1929, the year of Stresemann's death, took place in 1930.

Stresemann's second goal was to mobilize the so-called ethnic Germans, primarily those in Austria, Czechoslovakia, Poland, and the Balkans. He hoped that they would form German outposts in their countries, push them toward a pro-German political and economic course, and perhaps encourage their incorporation into Germany. There too he was successful, much more so than Hitler later on. After World War II, however, that policy was to spell disaster for these "ethnic Germans."

Stresemann's third goal, more long-range, was a territorial revision in the East, primarily the elimination of the so-called Polish Corridor. He also hoped one day to regain—through pressure, not necessarily through war—the Upper Silesian region that had become part of Poland. That did not seem a completely vain hope, considering that the Locarno Treaty tied France's hands in East Europe.

The fourth and most far-ranging of Stresemann's goals was the unification of Germany and

Austria. At the time Austria also favored *Anschluss*. Stresemann was willing to put off this part of his scheme until the diplomatic climate became more favorable.

Germany remained revisionist, but for the time being the only goal it pursued was the early evacuation of the Rhineland and a settlement of the reparations problem. The Young Plan, which made reparations a financial rather than a purely political matter, paved the way for such an agreement in 1929. It further reduced Germany's reparations debt and extended the repayment period to the 1980s. Since the German economy was flourishing, these obligations were easily met out of its trade surplus.

The worldwide economic crisis set off by the American stock market crash of 1929 shattered Germany's interval of comparative calm and prosperity. The consequences were very serious: American loan payments were suspended and short-term loans were rescinded altogether. German employment immediately declined; a wave of bankruptcies swept the country.

For the second time the German government was able to slough off the reparations burden, including the provisions of the Young Plan. This time, however, it was not going to be done via the kind of mass inflation of the twenties but via deflation. This ploy so impoverished the country that it simply was unable to make any further payments. Even its creditors ultimately had to face up to this stark fact.

This calculated deflation was the second great social catastrophe of the Weimar period, and this time the policy succeeded. In view of the worldwide economic crisis, all the countries involved, and the United States in particular, agreed that, given the existing situation, so-called political debts—loan repayments of its West European allies as well as Germany's reparations payments to the West European allies—must not be allowed to put any additional burden on the fragile world economy. In 1931 President Hoover proposed a moratorium on all such political payments, initially for one year. At the end of that year, France, England, and the other creditors signed an agreement in Lausanne permanently renouncing all further German reparations payments. They agreed upon one final lump payment of 3 billion marks, and even that was not a serious demand. In other words, Chancellor Heinrich Brüning's policy of impoverishing Germany to get out of paying reparations was successful, even though he himself was deposed shortly before it went into effect.

It is widely thought that the impoverishment of the years 1930 to 1933 was the inevitable byproduct of the world economic crisis. That, however, is only partially true, just as the inflation of 1919 to 1923 was only in part a consequence of a lost war financed by loans. A timely currency reform after the end of World War I would have spared Germany the expropriation of all savings, and a different economic policy could have substantially ameliorated the impact of the world economic crisis in Germany. Instead, the government exacerbated it. A policy of public expenditures through deficit spending to stimulate the economy, even at the risk of increasing the national debt, was advocated not only by Keynes but also by a number of German economists. Brüning's policy was the exact opposite. He exacerbated the consequences of the worldwide economic crisis by allowing the German economy to collapse in order to avoid paying reparations. As I said earlier, that part of his plan was successful. However, as we shall see, he helped drive the impoverished Germans into Hitler's arms.

That same year, German revisionism scored still another success. An international disarmament conference was held in Geneva in 1932. The Versailles Treaty had made the disarming of Germany a precondition for world disarmament. Germany now used this provision as a lever. It argued that the Western powers should either disarm to the same extent to which they had forced the Reich to disarm, or allow Germany to rearm. The argument succeeded. World opinion had changed, partly because of the economic crisis and partly because memories of World War I were beginning to fade. The mood had changed. In December 1932—Brüning had been replaced by

General Kurt von Schleicher—the Western powers at Geneva granted the Germans the right to rearm.

Thus, by the end of 1932, Germany via various routes had managed to shake off the two major obstacles to its resurgence—reparations and arms limitations. Now it once more stood as a major power among other major powers. As a matter of fact, as it turned out and as Locarno had underscored, in eastern and southeastern Europe Germany already was looked upon as a major power.

These were the great victories of German revisionism under the Weimar Republic, though ultimately they were to benefit an altogether different Germany.

By 1932 the Weimar Republic was internally exhausted, spent. The real political question no longer was whether it could be saved, but what would follow. In January 1933, soon after winning its last great victory, the republic fell to Hitler. And the Germany that regained its position as a major power, as a more-or-less hegemonic power at least in Eastern and Central Europe, was the Germany of Hitler.

7

The Hindenburg Era

THE PRECEDING CHAPTER dealt mainly with Versailles, not Weimar, or rather with Weimar's foreign policy and revisionism, not its domestic policy. Yet in the final analysis it was the domestic policy that led from Weimar to Hitler.

The Weimar Republic lasted a mere fourteen years, but in that brief span it went through three distinctive stages. In its early years, from its founding to 1924, it seemed destined to fail. Surprisingly enough, this stage was followed by a period of apparent consolidation, the "golden twenties," 1925 to 1929, and they in turn were followed by a period of disintegration, from 1930 to 1932, which paved the way for Hitler's takeover.

I will refrain from discussing the first period in detail. The years from 1920 to 1923, and in part also 1924, were an extraordinarily confused time replete with a succession of governments, putsch attempts by both the right and the left, and political assassinations largely by the right. And all this was played out against the backdrop of inflation, the first of the two great social catastrophes the republic created in the effort to rid itself of onerous reparations. Perhaps none of these events by itself was of world-shaking significance, yet two factors deserve closer scrutiny.

To begin with, the Weimar Republic was propped up by the three parties of the old Reichstag majority of 1917, the Social Democrats, the German Democratic Party, and the Center. They held a two-thirds majority in the National Assembly of 1919 and formed the Weimar Coalition. They were the only ones to vote for the Weimar Constitution and for replacing the monarchy, a form of government Germans had come to accept, with a republic. And even within these groupings there were many who did not actively favor the new form of government. They merely tolerated it. As a popular saying had it, Germany was a republic without republicans. This may have been hyperbole, but in fact the republic was precariously balanced on but one leg. The left Centrists were the only ones who actually liked the republic. The Communist left wanted an entirely different kind of republic. And the right, which in fact was far stronger than their representation in the National Assembly would indicate, simply wanted their kaiser back.

In the first Reichstag elections in the mid-1920s the Weimar coalition lost its majority position in the National Assembly. The Social Democrats lost almost half their seats, and the two other partners also suffered significant losses. The right regained its traditional strength. Consequently the German Reich never again had a stable government. There were minority governments of the non-Socialist parties and there were attempts at majority coalitions from left to right that fell apart as soon as they were formed. At one time, from the end of 1922 until August 1923, there even was a rightist government of so-called *Fachminister*, departmental ministers. All these governments were short-lived improvisations. That is the first factor that seemed to seal the fate of the fledgling republic.

The second is not so obvious. It has to do with the SPD, the major party in both the Weimar Coalition and the Weimar Republic, and the only one not free to change its course. Programmatically it had always been a republican party, but without openly saying so it had adjusted to the monarchy under William II. In 1918, when everything was falling apart, the SPD had offered to jump into the breach. On November 9, 1918, Ebert still attempted to save the monarchy by appointing a regent. When that failed the Social Democrats were ready to administer the republic like the old monarchy. They were willing to preserve the infrastructure of the monarchy, to let the ruling classes rule, to continue, so to speak, the monarchy under Social Democratic management—a very generous offer on the part of President Ebert to a society and state that he had taken over and saved from revolution. But his offer was rejected, and that epitomizes the enormous problems that beset the republic from the outset. All the institutions of the monarchy—army, bureaucracy, judiciary, church, universities, agriculture, industry—rejected the republic even though it never interfered with them. Their traditions and personnel, their status and positions, were never touched.

The rejection by these groups differed in degree. The top bureaucracy, the ministerial bureaucracy, remained grudgingly loyal. The ministerial counsels and administrative heads carried on; they made themselves useful, even if not with their wonted enthusiasm. They did their job. As a matter of fact their passive resistance helped foil one of the early rightist coups, the Kapp Putsch of 1920.

That was the most positive response to the republic on the part of the old elite. Unlike the upper bureaucracy, the Reichswehr during the Kapp Putsch maintained a position of icy neutrality toward both the legitimate and illegitimate governments. "Soldiers do not shoot at soldiers," proclaimed the commander in chief, General von Seeckt. At a later occasion, in another crisis, President Ebert, the army's nominal commander in chief, asked Seeckt a demeaning question: "I would really like to know where the Reichswehr stands on this," he said. "The Reichswehr stands behind me," was the arrogant reply.

At the secondary schools and universities the attitude toward the republic was extremely negative. Students and professors, teachers and pupils, as I know from personal experience, were antirepublicans, monarchists, nationalists, and revanchists. The situation in the churches was not quite that bad, but all in all the Protestant churches were as rightist then as they are leftist now. And the Catholic Church also distanced itself from the republic, even though the Catholic Center party was part of the government. In 1933 the Church changed course and signed a concordat with Hitler.

With regard to industry things were a little more complicated. Shortly after the revolution, in November, employers and unions signed an agreement, the so-called Stinnes-Legien Agreement, a sort of truce granting the unions a voice in wage negotiations. But inflation sharpened the class conflict between employers and workers. On the whole, Weimar was the republic of only one segment of the population, the workers (or at least of those who were not Communists); before too long business did not want any part of that state.

The rejection by these assorted groups was probably the biggest single reason why the republic failed to consolidate itself as a stable form of government of the German Reich under Ebert's presidency, from 1919 to 1924. The fact that Ebert, contrary to the provisions of the Weimar Constitution, was not elected but only "provisionally" appointed by the National Assembly, is secondary.

Then, between 1925 and 1929, it suddenly seemed as though the republic might yet succeed in consolidating itself. Ebert died in February 1925, and now for the first time the German people cast their ballots in a constitutional presidential election. The first round, in which every party fielded a candidate, produced no clear-cut winner. In the second round the German National party, the monarchist right, made a brilliant move. They ran a war hero, Field Marshal Hindenburg, as their candidate. He won.

Hindenburg's victory was a blow to the republicans. The aged war hero was fronting for the arch-reactionary Ludendorff, a dyed-in-the-wool monarchist. How would the republic fare under him? Surprisingly enough, things went very well for a while. The first five years of Hindenburg's presidency turned out to be the best period of the Weimar Republic. Finally everything seemed to be coming together, and for a simple reason.

The old ruling classes of the monarchy who continued to be the real rulers of the Republic without ever accepting the new state now took a fresh look. A republic presided over by Hindenburg, a highly respected figure of the monarchy, a man who in World War I had already been a sort of surrogate emperor, was something altogether different from Ebert and the Social Democrats. Consequently the biggest rightist party of the Reichstag, the German National People's party, which up to then had refused to participate in the government, changed its mind.

Between 1925 and 1928, the Weimar Republic was governed almost uninterruptedly by a rightist majority coalition of the Center, the German People's party, and the German Nationalists. Now the Republic was firmly planted on two legs. It no longer depended on a center-left coalition. A coalition of the Center and the right took over and stabilized the country.

Furthermore, as we have seen, the economic situation improved palpably in those years. In the last year of Ebert's life inflation had been halted, currency reform, even a modest revaluation, had finally come, and, thanks to the flow of American loans, there even was a mini-prosperity. Foreign policy was also able to chalk up some successes: the evacuation of the Ruhr, followed by the Locarno Treaty, a sort of belated Western peace accord which insured against any possible French attacks. In short, the future looked promising, and until 1928 it looked as though good times were here to stay.

Then two things happened even before the market crash of 1929 that destabilized the republic once again. The first was the mid-1928 electoral defeat of the ruling center-right coalition. The German Nationalists lost votes and the Social Democrats scored their greatest victory since 1919. This meant that no new government could be formed, neither on the basis of the old Weimar Coalition nor on the basis of what I call the Hindenburg Coalition. The Weimar Republic lacked something the present-day Federal Republic has had from the very beginning: a clear-cut party alignment of the right and the left. Weimar had to fall back on a so-called Great Coalition of the left and the right, from the SPD all the way to the right Liberals, and that was a very weak government because its two wings pulled it in different directions. The period from mid-1928 to early 1930, the time of the Great Coalition, lacked political stability despite the favorable economic situation.

That was one destabilizing factor. The other, which proved to be far more dangerous, had to do with the person of the president. In 1925, when he took office, Hindenburg was seventy-seven years old; by now he was more than eighty. He would not be president forever. It was not to be assumed that in 1932, after seven years in office and at the age of eighty-four, he would be able to run for office again, let alone serve out a full term. What was to be done? There was no second Hindenburg in sight. The fate of that wonderful compromise worked out in the early Hindenburg years, the near-monarchist republic that the monarchist right was ready to accept, rested on aged shoulders.

How could this compromise be saved—or should it be saved at all? The right grew restless. The German Nationalists had a new, far more radical leadership and no longer were part of the government. They began to reassess their attitude toward the Hindenburg era. Perhaps, they told themselves, it should be seen not as the stabilizer of the republic but as the transition to the restoration of the monarchy. Could Hindenburg gradually evolve from president of the Reich into trustee, perhaps even regent, of a restored monarchy? Plans of this sort were seriously discussed in the army and given substance by its leading political figure, General von Schleicher.

In the spring of 1929, before the economic crash, in a time of seeming calm and stability, Schleicher invited the new rightist leader of the Center party, Heinrich Brüning, to his house. The general, as we have since learned from Brüning's memoirs, made suggestions that seemed to invite a coup.

The balance of the old chancellor's term,

Schleicher told Brüning, must be utilized to revise the constitution, to clip the wings of the Reichstag and bring back the "stable conditions" of the unreformed monarchy of the pre–October 1918 days. Not only should the head of state—a monarch was not yet mentioned—have the power to appoint the chancellor, but he must also have the power to keep him in office, against the will of the Reichstag if need be. This would keep the parliament in its place and prevent it from interfering with policymaking, like in the good old days of the monarchy. This scheme might necessitate periodic dissolutions of the Reichstag, until the parties grew so tired and financially so depleted that they stopped holding elections. And then, in one of those periods without a Reichstag, the constitution could be changed into a purely presidential document in which the president would be given the role of the former emperor.

Brüning was interested. He asked Schleicher how long he thought all this would take. Schleicher believed one ought to be able to do it in half a year. He also confided to Brüning that the president had taken a liking to him, the loyal frontline officer whose machine-gun company had fought with distinction until the very end, and that he was considering entrusting him, Brüning, with the task of carrying out such a coup. The time was not yet ripe for this plan, but it came quickly.

The worldwide economic crisis began in October 1929, the month of Stresemann's untimely death. The government of the Great Coalition he had headed could not cope with the deteriorating situation. It collapsed, and in March 1930 Hindenburg on Schleicher's recommendation made Brüning chancellor. Brüning invoked Article 48 of the constitution, which empowered a head of state to circumvent the law-making functions of the Reichstag and govern by emergency decree if he deemed it necessary. The president himself had the right to dissolve the Reichstag, so in the event that the parliament rescinded any of the emergency decrees, the president could simply dissolve it. Brüning was now to exercise all of these powers on behalf of the president, the interim step in the restoration of the monarchy plotted by the people behind Hindenburg.

It is not clear what role Hindenburg himself played in all this. The old man was no politician and never had been. In many respects he was still the same figurehead he had been when he was the wartime chief of the Supreme Command. But he had his own agenda, always had had, and with age he grew even more stubborn. He had kept his oath of office to uphold the constitution, and he enjoyed the honors that had come to him. However, once he was in office, his monarchist feelings probably resurfaced, and he may have persuaded himself that it was his mission to retransform the republic into the monarchy—if possible without directly violating his oath of office. The first step was the transition from the parliamentary government of the twenties to the presidential governments of the early thirties, of which Brüning's was the first and most durable. Formally it still moved within the framework of the constitution, which explains the paradox of Brüning's reputation as the last defender of the Weimar Constitution. He was not. He was called in to stage a coup, as he himself wrote in his memoirs, and he was more than willing to carry out his assignment. He put it off in favor of another plan, however, and that ultimately led to his downfall.

When the world economic crisis broke out, Brüning saw it as his big chance to realize one of his foreign-policy goals; he saw the chance to exploit the situation to get rid of Germany's burdensome reparations by exacerbating the crisis. He felt that this took precedence over the planned coup. Be that as it may, in July 1930 he dissolved the Reichstag and scheduled new elections for September. However, something unexpected happened. Hitler's National Socialists, which in the good old Hindenburg days had been nothing but a splinter party, suddenly emerged as the second-strongest party, winning six million votes, or 18 percent of the total, giving them 107 parliamentary seats. With that a new force emerged on the domestic political scene, one to be reckoned with. What accounted for the sudden strength of the National Socialists?

Three factors combined to turn the National

Socialists into a mass party in 1930 and into the strongest party in 1932.

The first is the economic crisis and the consequent precipitous decline in the standard of living of workers and employers alike. In 1932, a year that saw unemployment climb to six million, a poster was plastered all over Germany showing a mass of huddled miserable figures, with the simple caption, HITLER, OUR LAST HOPE. It sent a clear message. Poverty had become a fact of life. And it was also a fact that Hitler was the only one who held out hope for a change, whereas Brüning seemed intent on making things even worse—for reasons of patriotism and foreign-policy goals he could not make public and which even today are not generally understood.

Widespread misery is the explanation most frequently given for Hitler's mass support, the one overriding reason for the sudden mass appeal of the Nazis. It was indeed a reason, a very persuasive one, but not the only one.

A second reason, neither as obvious nor as easy to understand, was the resurgence of nationalism. One might ask why this should have happened in a time of economic crisis, but it did happen, and all who lived through that period know it only too well. The national feelings and resentments of the post-1918 years, catchwords like "stab-in-the-back" and "November criminals," had never been completely forgotten, except that from 1919 to 1924 they had been the exclusive property of the old rightists, the voters of the German Nationalist People's Party, and after 1925, when the party joined the government, they were muted. Now suddenly they became part of everyday political discourse. Even the Communists began to speak in nationalistic tones; the secret and overt monarchists supporting Brüning's presidential cabinet had never stopped. But in joining in the chorus the Communists became involved in something of which the National Socialists were the masters. Nobody could match the fervor and intensity of their appeal to nationalism, to national pride and national resentments. No one else dared claim, as they did, that Germany could have won the war, or had in fact won it, only to have victory snatched away by cunning and betrayal. No one dared say as openly as they did that this loss would have to be avenged one day. The Germans in 1939—I am now anticipating—were not nearly as enthusiastic about that war as about the war of 1914. They had spent their passion in 1933. Their jubilation over the "national reawakening" in 1933 rivaled their enthusiasm of 1914. A sort of war frenzy had been stirred up in the preceding years, and the National Socialists cashed in on it.

The third reason for the electoral success of the Nazis is the persona of Hitler himself. That must be said even if today people would rather not hear it. The Germans of that time were not repelled by Hitler. On the contrary, they found him charismatic. He was a figure of much greater political appeal than any of the others who appeared on the scene in the closing days of the Weimar Republic, after Stresemann's death.

Hitler was underestimated. The biggest mistake his enemies made was to treat him with disdain, to ridicule him. Hitler was a truly evil man, not an insignificant, ridiculous one. Great men are often evil. And Hitler, despite all his horrifying attributes, was a great man, as he demonstrated over and over again by the boldness of his vision and the cunning of his instincts. Hitler had a magic touch, and none of his adversaries could compete with him.

In 1918 and 1919 many Germans were dreaming of a man like Hitler, a tough and cunning leader able to bring order to the country, discipline the people, put an end to party rule, take hold of the reins, and know what to do, particularly in the area of foreign policy and, yes, war. It was a dream that had never really died, and in 1930 it suddenly flared up again. Hitler seemed the one to make it all come true. For many Germans Hitler represented an ideal: his eloquence, his brutality, his toughness, his steadfastness, his talent for the unexpected, his ability to get out of tight spots. His anti-Semitism? Well, many were willing to go along with it.

Three factors—misery, a resurgent nationalism, and Hitler himself—made the National Socialists into a mass movement that appropriated and nurtured and transformed the party into a po-

171

litical power. The German rightist establishment, the elitist right which had again come to power under Hindenburg, could not ignore it.

Schleicher, the guiding spirit of the restoration movement, was well aware of this. He tried to push Brüning to preempt Hitler and carry out the monarchist coup before Hitler could overwhelm them. But Brüning hesitated; Schleicher called him "Brüning Cunctator." Brüning's priority was his big foreign-policy coup: getting rid of the reparations. And that needed time. The reparations were not written off until July 1932, but by then Brüning was already gone.

Before that Brüning had found a way of continuing to govern in a semiparliamentary fashion. At the end of 1930 he had suddenly managed to put together a parliamentary majority. The Social Democrats, stunned by Hitler's rise, had decided to tolerate Brüning as the lesser of two evils—that is, to get him a majority in the Reichstag without themselves becoming part of the government. Brüning, even had he wanted to, would not have been allowed to take any Social Democrats into his government. He was, after all, the head of a presidential government; he did not want a parliamentary government. But he accepted the Social Democrats' support and governed fairly uneventfully, with his quasiparliamentary majority and his emergency decrees, until 1932, always in the hope that once he had chalked up his great foreign-policy victory he could attack the domestic changes that had been his real assignment. But Schleicher had lost patience. He persuaded Hindenburg to get rid of Brüning and replace him with someone who would do what Brüning was supposed to have done: clear the way for a new, authoritarian constitution. The man Schleicher more or less invented to fill that role was Franz von Papen, a practically unknown Center party deputy in the Prussian legislature. Moreover, Papen, unlike the middle-class Brüning, was a typical representative of the old Wilhelmine ruling class.

In June 1932 the new chancellor appointed his cabinet, the "Cabinet of the Barons," as it soon came to be called, and promised "an entirely new type of governmental and national leadership." Unlike Brüning, Papen immediately started on the road to the coup d'état. He began by dissolving the Reichstag. At the end of July elections were held, and with 37 percent of the vote the Nazis became the strongest party in Germany. The Communists also scored substantial gains. The Reichstag of July 1932 was the first one unable to put together a working majority of middle-of-the-road parties and Social Democrats. Now the two revolutionary antigovernment parties, the National Socialists on the right and the Communists on the left, together were the majority, but of course they could not put this to practical use. So Papen found himself in a very favorable position as far as the planned coup was concerned, since the Reichstag obviously and clearly was not capable of governing.

Papen promptly dissolved the Reichstag, although not before an overwhelming majority had expressed its lack of confidence in him. The dissolution of the Reichstag was a clear violation of the constitution, because according to the constitution a chancellor who had received a vote of no confidence automatically had to resign. Papen, of course, had no such intention.

This was not Papen's first violation of the constitution. He had violated it once before, soon after his appointment, when he dismissed the legitimate Prussian government, which was still a part of the Weimar Coalition, had the ministers forcibly ejected from their offices by the army, and named himself Reich commissar of Prussia. That had been a minor coup (and from the perspective of history it was also the real end of Prussia's independence). In the absence of the Reichstag, Papen planned to go ahead with the coup by invoking Article 48 and change the democratic constitution into a monarchist one. That was what Papen intended to do, and Hindenburg stood ready to support him. Now it was Schleicher who left Papen in the lurch.

Papen's, Hindenburg's, and Schleicher's original idea of a monarchist revolution had one major flaw: No candidate for the throne was in sight. It was not possible to bring back Emperor William II from his exile in Holland. His ignominious flight had cost him the respect of all the people, including the monarchists. He could not possibly be put

174

back on the throne, even though that was Hindenburg's personal preference.

The crown prince had withdrawn into private life after his return to Germany, and so he too was not a feasible candidate. His sons were young and unknown. In all of Germany there was only one man who could possibly be considered a serious contender: Crown Prince Rupprecht of Bavaria. His fellow Bavarians would undoubtedly have liked to see him crowned king of Bavaria. But making him the new German emperor would involve the restored monarchy in a dynastic change. That posed a grave problem. Papen, Hindenburg, and Schleicher ultimately came up with the idea of making the reelected president regent on behalf of a son of the crown prince. But in view of Hindenburg's age, that solution too was rejected. The German people would not have accepted it. That left only a coup supported by the aged Hindenburg, and no one knew what would happen once he was gone. Moreover, such a coup was likely to encounter a sizable group of opponents: the powerful, popular Nazi movement, the remnants of republicans, and the still-powerful Communists. Military force would probably have been needed, and that might have brought on a general strike and public unrest. Schleicher got cold feet. He did not want to govern against all those other groups, and he had learned, as would Papen, that the National Socialists were not at all inclined to accede to or tolerate the restoration of the monarchy.

Hitler wanted all power for himself, nor were his thirteen million voters waiting for a return to the monarchy and the old Wilhelmine system. They wanted something new and dynamic. It is probably fair to say that they wanted what they finally got: Hitler's autocratic rule. In the electoral battles of 1932, first in the presidential election in which Hitler opposed Hindenburg, then in the Reichstag elections of July 31, and finally in the second Reichstag election of November, the National Socialists no longer ran only against the "November criminals" but essentially against the old-new ruling class, against the "barons," against Papen. The National Socialists were always oscillating between right and left. In 1932 they stressed their "left," populist side. In November 1932 they even joined forces with the Communists in the Berlin transport workers' strike. A picture taken at the time shows Joseph Goebbels and Walter Ulbricht sharing a platform.

Schleicher decided that the Reichswehr was no match for such an alliance. He had had a change of heart after acquiring a brain trust of brilliant young journalists, the publishers of a popular monthly, *Die Tat*. They persuaded him to revise his simple restorative notions of 1929 and try to forge an alliance of the army, the trade unions, and the youth organizations as the base on which to build a future government. Furthermore, he decided to try and split the National Socialists, to invite Gregor Strasser, the Nazi organizational expert, into the government and bring a portion of the party with him. What Schleicher had in mind was a sort of corporate state, something like a German fascism, to undermine Hitler. The restoration of the monarchy played only a minor role in these new Schleicher plans. Perhaps he had even decided to discard them. But whatever his reason, Schleicher no longer went along with Papen's coup plans of late November, and he toppled him. A very reluctant Hindenburg was forced to go along and appoint Schleicher chancellor.

During Schleicher's brief chancellorship all his plans collapsed. Once exposed to the light of day, this political general, the most powerful figure in Germany as long as he was operating behind the scenes, turned out to be the most luckless German chancellor ever. Nothing worked for him. The trade unions refused to cooperate, Gregor Strasser failed him, and the support of the youth alone was not enough. An anti-Schleicher faction formed even in the Reichswehr. The National Socialists, who had lost two million votes in the November election, bounced back, and the Communists also gained.

At the end of January, Schleicher had to do something he might possibly still have been able to avoid in November: ask Hindenburg to dissolve the Reichstag and allow him to form a government without parliamentary consent—in other words, to stage a coup. But that which Hindenburg had given to Papen two months earlier he now refused to Schleicher.

Hindenburg had kept in touch with Papen, who now had his ear, and Papen for his part had not been inactive. He had always toyed with the idea of somehow using Hitler. Back in August 1932 he had even thought of making him his vice chancellor—which only showed that not only did he underestimate Hitler, he had no inkling of what made him tick.

Papen saw Hitler from the vantage point of the elite. He considered him a gifted plebeian, a climber who would be happy to be a valet in the Cabinet of the Barons. He had no idea of Hitler's far grander, far more ambitious plans.

Hitler turned down Papen's magnanimous offer. He insisted on the chancellorship and complete presidential powers. Hitler wanted his own coup. Papen revised his mistaken notion of what Hitler wanted and decided that if need be he could even live with those conditions. Papen felt confident that even if Hitler were to become the nominal chancellor and he himself Hitler's vice chancellor, the real power would still rest with the president. If Hitler could be co-opted, as Papen put it, if he did not insist on moving in on the government lock, stock, and barrel, if he showed himself willing to form a coalition with the German Nationalists and perhaps even with the Center, then why not?

When the coalition of the National Socialists and German Nationalists was formed at the end of January 1933, Papen smugly told an appalled, astonished critic who accused him of having brought Hitler to power, "You'll be surprised. We hired him." How wrong he was!

8

The Hitler Era

THE LAST ERA OF THE GER-
man Reich must be called the Hitler era, although
that designation does not hint at what differen-
tiates it from two previous eras—the pre–World
War I Imperial era or the Hindenburg era of the
dying Weimar Republic.

Even though the emperor and Hindenburg
were the representative figures of their respective
eras, they could not single-handedly impose either
domestic or foreign policies on the German Reich.

Bismarck possibly might have, but even he could not dominate or shape his era as relentlessly and completely as did Hitler in the final twelve years of his rule.

When Hitler was made chancellor on January 30, 1933, he did not immediately arrogate all power to himself. On the contrary. At the time there were still many who thought that the curious Hitler-Papen government would collapse as quickly as its predecessors and be succeeded by something altogether different. That this did not happen may have come as a surpise to many, and perhaps even as a welcome surprise.

Within four months of becoming chancellor, Hitler had taken complete charge of Germany's political life, and by the end of July 1933 his tight grip on the reins of power was absolute. His take-over thus was a two-stage process.

The first half of 1933 was the first phase, which he used to clear the political arena. On January 30, 1933, the mixture of remnants of Weimar parliamentary democracy and the new authoritarian presidential rule that had evolved over the past three years still prevailed. By July 14, 1933, it had become a thing of the past. The political parties disappeared, as did presidential and parliamentary rule. The chancellor and his party now were the sole ruling forces. The way for this was cleared by an audacious move involving countless violations of law and unprecedented violence.

The crucial event, although some of the details are still somewhat murky, was the Reichstag fire on February 27, 1933. Hitler, with Papen's concurrence, used this act of arson as a pretext to induce the president to sign an emergency decree granting him unlimited powers. The constitution was more or less suspended, all basic rights were nullified, and arbitrary arrests became the order of the day. All this had been well prepared and took effect immediately, on February 28.

A new feature was introduced into German political life: legalized state terror. Initially the terror was used fairly selectively. The first victims were the Communists and other left-wing political figures, primarily leftist journalists and writers who had incurred the displeasure of the ruling clique. In the first weeks terror was not yet widespread, but it nevertheless had crucial consequences. The eighty-one Communist delegates elected the week after the fire were no longer in a position to take their seats in the newly elected Reichstag when it met three weeks later. They either had been sent to concentration camps or had gone underground or emigrated. That effectively nullified the election results.

The election had not pleased the government. The National Socialists and the German Nationalists won only a slim combined majority of 52 percent; the National Socialists by themselves received only 42.9 percent of the votes cast, instead of their hoped-for absolute majority. But once the Communist deputies were gone, the National Socialists suddenly had an absolute majority, and together with the non-Socialist parties they even had the two-thirds majority they needed for the ultimate revision of the constitution—the dissolution of the Reichstag.

This two-thirds majority was forged on March 23, when the question of the abrogation of the parliamentary constitution was put to a vote. All parties except the Social Democrats voted for the so-called Enabling Act, which allowed the government to "legally" promulgate laws without the consent of the Reichstag, initially for a period of four years. That was the second coup after the arson of February 28. From there it was only a short step to the self-immolation of all non-Socialist parties and the banning of the Social Democratic and Communist parties in June and July.

One of the most striking aspects of this period is the ready acquiescence of the non-Socialist parties, their withdrawal from political life. This is connected to what at the time was called the "nationalist awakening" or the "National Socialist revolution"—that is, a complete change in popular mood between the Reichstag elections of March 5 and the summer of 1933. It is something that cannot be documented, but anyone who was there remembers it well. It is difficult to pinpoint moods; they are atmospheric, ephemeral, but they are significant. The popular mood played as great a role then as in August 1914, because this change in public feeling created the real power base for the future Führer state. It was—there is no other way of putting it—a widespread feeling of deliverance, of liberation from democracy. What should a democracy do when a majority of its people no longer values it? At the time most of the democratic politicians chose to resign and abandon politics, as though they were saying, "If that's what you want you can have it." In June and July 1933 the democratic parties behaved just as the crown prince had in November 1918.

The "national awakening"—and I remember it very clearly—had twin roots. The first was the dismay over the political uncertainty of the preceding years. People wanted to know where they stood; they wanted order, a firm hand, a strong will, a man to lead them. But, and that is the other root of that movement, they did not want a man like Papen or Schleicher, a representative of the effete old monarchist elite of 1918. They wanted someone entirely new, a popular leader (as Hitler appeared to be), and above all they wanted Germany once more to be unified, great, and strong— as in 1914, when the kaiser told them, "I don't know any parties anymore, I only know Germans." Now they really did not want parties anymore, only Germans. In doing away with the parties, Hitler won the support of a majority of the non-Socialist electorate, not only those who had voted for his National Socialists on March 5.

This national mood made an indelible impression on the representatives of the old non-Socialist parties. A former minister of the Weimar Republic and now a delegate of the left-liberal Democratic party, who after some misgivings voted for the Enabling Act, said after 1945 that never before had he received so many letters of approbation from his constituents as after that particular vote. This may not seem all that significant, but it was symptomatic of a growing tendency between March and July 1933. Despite all the lawlessness of that period, despite the concentration camps and arbitrary arrests, despite the first unmistakable signs of official anti-Semitism, there was a growing sense that great times lay ahead. Once again the country would close ranks and find a savior, a man of the people, a leader who would restore discipline and order, who would unify the nation and lead the German Reich toward new and better days. It was this mood that enabled Hitler to clear the political stage with little resistance and to create an atmosphere in which no one outside his ranks would be able to stand up against him or thwart his plans.

It is a process that is still not fully understood, probably because people like to forget that in the spring and early summer of 1933 something like a national coming together was indeed taking place, not necessarily behind the National Socialist Party, but behind Hitler, behind the Führer, as he was beginning to be called. And simultaneously another extraordinary process was taking place, the so-called *Gleichschaltung,* the "leveling," bringing all aspects of life into line. All political or even nonpolitical organizations (other than the parties then still in existence), from industrial associations to trade unions down to the smallest local clubs, made every effort to fall in step, in other words to change their leadership, to become part of and go along with the movement that was sweeping through Germany.

In addition, vast numbers who had had no truck with the National Socialists rushed to join the party, the NSDAP, before it closed its doors to new applicants. There was one brief period in 1937 when new members were admitted into the party, and once again many non–National Socialist pragmatists eager to get ahead in their careers joined up—a not particularly admirable though all-too-human act. But regardless of their motives, the Germans in the thirties became a politically unified nation.

Now to the second phase of the takeover. What did things look like once the political stage had been cleared and Hitler and his party were the sole political power in Germany? The National Socialist party may have been the only *political* power, but it was not the *only* power. Hitler's establishment encompassed a number of other instruments, among them most importantly its defense corps, the SA.

Initially the SA was the real instrument of the official terror. The first concentration camps were set up and run by the SA, and at times it seemed as though it were an independent terror regime. It did not make arrests only when ordered by higher authorities, it also made arrests on its own, and not infrequently because of personal animus. To some extent Hitler had lost control over the terror and its physical violence and murders.

In addition to the SA there was another power center, not a political one but a much more real one: the Reichswehr. The army at first had supported Hitler's elevation to the chancellorship. A new group in the High Command, one committed not to General von Schleicher but to Generals Werner von Blomberg and Walther von Reichenau, was friendly toward the Nazis and thought it could use them for their own purposes, so they had supported Hindenburg when he made Hitler chancellor in January. However, the Reichswehr remained what it had always been—a state within the state. It was a friendly ally of the Nazis but not their subordinate.

A conflict with the potential of embarrassing Hitler broke out between the Reichswehr and the SA. The SA, a mass organization commanded by World War I noncoms, had visions of becoming the new Reichswehr, the great new revolutionary National Socialist army of the new Reich, in part by replacing the old Reichswehr leadership or by incorporating it into the SA, and in part by pensioning them off. One might think that this was in keeping with Hitler's ideas, considering that the

SA was his organization and that he was its supreme leader. Under this scenario, he would have a politically reliable army under his direct command rather than one that merely supported him. Yet Hitler sided with the Reichswehr, for two reasons, it seems to me. The less important one was that from day one Hitler had planned to rearm and go to war. It was surely no accident that the first group he addressed in early February 1933, immediately after becoming chancellor, was the General Staff of the Reichswehr. For his rearmament and future war Hitler needed not only a willing instrument, but, above all, a trained, first-rate force. And the Reichswehr was just that. The SA, with its millions of enthusiastic lower-class members, lacked the military esprit and tradition of the Reichswehr. But Hitler had another, even more important reason for siding with the army in its contest with the SA.

Although Hindenburg was still alive, he no longer was as politically powerful as before. He was extremely old, and in 1934 he withdrew to his estate at Neubeck. Who would succeed him? Hitler was determined to be the one, to consummate his takeover by assuming the combined offices of chancellor and president. That however could be done only if the army put no obstacle in his way. Hitler thus was forced to try to obtain an agreement with the Reichswehr that would allow him to assume the presidency. In the final analysis, such an agreement would put the Reichswehr under the direct command of the new president, in this case Hitler, for the head of state was also the commander in chief of the armed forces.

The Reichswehr agreed to hand Hitler this all-important prize if he in turn would rescind the planned takeover of the army by the SA and refrain from using the SA as his instrument of terror. That put Hitler in a very difficult position. There is considerable evidence to support the theory that he had led the SA to believe that after Hindenburg's death they would get a chance to carry out their "second revolution," the military revolution. Hitler saw only one way out of this dilemma: to murder the leadership of the SA. And that is what he did on June 30, 1934. One does not have to be unduly sympathetic to the SA to be appalled by what happened to them.

In anticipation of Hindenburg's expected death, Hitler had granted the SA collective leave for the month of July. At the same time he said he wished to meet with its leadership at Bad Wiessee on June 30 in order to make plans for the future. The SA leaders arrived at Wiessee on June 29; Hitler was expected the next morning. However, he got to Wiessee sometime during the night under heavy police escort, not with the intention of holding a meeting but rather to have the assembled leadership arrested and shipped off to Munich or Berlin, where they were executed without trial and without warning. He later claimed he had had to act to prevent a planned putsch. And in fact history texts still speak of the so-called Röhm Putsch.

But there never was such a putsch. In planning the military coup, Ernst Röhm, the SA's chief of staff, thought he was carrying out Hitler's orders. Instead, he, along with most of the other leaders, was arrested in his sleep and later murdered. A few days later the cabinet put its stamp of approval on the events of June 30 by saying that Hitler had acted in defense of the state. This was a foretaste of the murderous, arbitrary reign of terror that was to engulf Germany from 1938 to 1945.

The Reichswehr honored its agreement with Hitler. Hindenburg died on August 2, and on that same day Hitler named himself Hindenburg's successor. The Reichswehr swore allegiance to Hitler as their new commander in chief. With that, Hitler neutralized the military and turned himself into both the political and military center of power, something on the order of a supreme general, a new emperor.

On the whole, the German people and the old elite supported the horrifying murder of the SA leadership, perhaps not as unreservedly as they had approved of the elimination of the political parties, yet still with a measure of satisfaction and relief. The SA had not been very popular. The upper classes had looked on them as proletarian rabble, and the middle class had feared them because their unpredictable and brutal excesses affected all areas of life, including business. They welcomed the fact that the Führer had put a stop to all of this, that they could now look forward to a return to normalcy, never mind the methods used. And the fact that Hitler used the occasion to rid himself of a number of prominent conservatives, including his predecessor, General von Schleicher, and Schleicher's wife, also did not raise too many eyebrows. If one can speak of the collective guilt of the German people, then perhaps this is where it all began.

The two political upheavals of those early Hitler years, the one from March to July 1933 and the other from June to August 1934, were followed by a period of calm that lasted until the fall of 1938. They were the so-called "good" Nazi years. During that time the terror of the early years was more or less held in check. Of course, the concentration camps were still in operation, but their population decreased; more were let out than were sent in. Life appeared to be returning to normal.

At the same time, Hitler's economic miracle was taking off. The economy was reinvigorated. In the four years from 1933 to 1937 Germany went from mass unemployment to full employment. With this Hitler won the support of—or at least neutralized—the overwhelming majority of former Social Democrats and a large number of former Communists. It remains an open question, however, to what extent the German people really stood behind Hitler. He had never won an absolute majority in a free election, and the 99 percent he got in the various plebiscites and Reichstag elections between November 1933 and the spring of 1938 are meaningless. They were not real elections. The people had to vote if they did not want to call attention to themselves, and so they simply dropped their ballots in the box. It made no difference whether those ballots were blank or not. Still, no one who was there at the time can deny that by the end of 1933 or 1934 at the latest, Hitler was supported by the vast majority of the German people. They approved of his rule and of the results he got. The middle class liked his program of rearmament and his equally successful defiant stance in foreign affairs, and the workers liked the unexpected economic upturn and the jobs they won.

What kind of state was Germany during that time? Contrary to widely held beliefs it was not a one-party state, unlike today's German Democratic Republic or the Soviet Union, which are dominated by a highly structured political party. The National Socialist party had no central committee, no Politburo, and Hitler never convened executive committee meetings. The annual party congresses staged at Nuremberg with great fanfare were not the sort of congresses at which delegates meet to discuss issues and vote on programs. No such meetings were ever held. The Nazi party congresses were public displays of organizational muscle. Special days were dedicated to the various groupings: a Day of the SA, a Day of the SS, a Day of the Reich Labor Service, and after 1934 also a

Day of the Wehrmacht (the new name of the German army after the introduction of universal military service). All organs, all segments of the state, were brought together for one huge, impressive demonstration at which Hitler, and only Hitler, addressed the masses. No one else spoke. It was not the party that dominated the state but Hitler who dominated everything, including the party.

Once all other parties had been eliminated the National Socialist party also ceased to play any meaningful role in Hitler's state. By now the names of almost all top regional and national officials, the party's highest functionaries, are forgotten, and even during the Third Reich they were largely unknown to the general population. Hitler's Third Reich was not a party state, it was a Führer state.

And contrary to popular belief, Germany also was not really a totalitarian state. Hitler's state, more than any other in the history of the German Reich, encompassed many different states. In his book *The Dual State*, the German émigré historian Ernst Fraenkel points out that the Third Reich was composed of at least two states: a state of arbitrary rule and terror alongside the old traditional, bureaucratic, even constitutional state. Civic disputes before the courts were handled as in the past. The same laws and the same legal procedures were followed, National Socialism notwithstanding. And the same holds true for many ministerial functions, where established procedures continued to be followed and where, particularly after 1934, when the terror of the SA had abated, a measure of normalcy was restored. Of course, it was a normalcy that could be interrupted any time the Führer chose to embark on a particular political campaign; he could always find the requisite instruments to carry out his will.

The Wehrmacht continued to function as a state within the state. The writer Gottfried Benn, who at the time returned to his original profession of military doctor, called it the aristocratic form of emigration.

Well, it was no emigration, and even the designation "aristocratic" is open to dispute. But it was a form of withdrawal, a retreat into a special niche, into a special state within the state, in which old traditions and customs continued to prevail. Thus, for example, the Hitler salute did not replace the traditional military salute until 1944.

The survival of such niches was by no means due to an oversight on the part of Hitler. The Nazis have been called a movement, but, strange as this may seem, after 1933 the only real movement was Hitler himself. Not only did he set the entire Reich and the entire population in motion, he never framed a new constitution, he never coordinated or integrated the numerous institutions and organizations he had created—and he did all this consciously, to keep everything in flux, because he did not look upon the German Reich as something definitive, as a legacy that had to be preserved. For Hitler the Reich was a launching pad, the point of departure for territorial expansion, a new power structure with a fuzzy internal constitutional framework. That accounts for the internal chaos of the Third Reich.

How did Hitler nonetheless manage to govern this nontotalitarian, highly departmentalized state as a Führer state? Given this "authoritarian anarchy" (as it has been called), how was it possible for a supreme authority to impose its will wherever and whenever it chose? The explanation can be found in two words: propaganda and terror. These two instruments were Hitler's most important tools from day one to the very end. They set the Hitler state apart from any of its predecessors.

Let us examine the terror first. To begin with, there were the concentration camps. Citizens could be sent there arbitrarily, without arrest warrants, without legal recourse, without indictment, and once there they could expect the worst. After the fall of the SA the camps came under the control of Hitler's other terror instrument, the SS. On June 30, 1934, Hitler made a very clever move. He did not ask the Reichswehr to carry out the execution of the SA leadership. They were only too glad not to have to soil their hands with this dirty job. Rather, he used another special force, the SS, then the special paramilitary section of the SA.

The requisite arms were furnished by the Reichswehr. With this single stroke the SS became both
the new SA and something else as well. Unlike
the SA, the SS was never a primarily political organization. From the very outset it was supposed
to represent a sort of aristocracy among National
Socialist organizations, a racially select troop with
"clean" family trees going back all the way to
1800. And it also had a special function. The SA
had hoped to become the Wehrmacht, and when
it was denied that role it dwindled into insignif-
icance. The SS had a different goal: It wanted to
become Germany's police, and it did. In the early
Hitler years the police were still under the jurisdiction of the individual states, but later were cen-
tralized under a new national department—the
Central Reich Security Office. In no time at all it
came under the total control of the SS whose top
leaders took over the police, and police officials
were given SS ranks. The SS and the police fused
into a single entity, which made them an important new power in the state.

The SS continued to spread its wings. Their
acts of terror, which were separate from their
equally feared police functions, were carried out
by special units, the so-called Death Head com-
panies. They replaced the SA as the overseers and
managers of the concentration camps and imposed
a much more impersonal, more predictable, and
more disciplined, though certainly not more hu-

mane, regimen. They were far harsher and more punitive. The penalty for trivial infractions of the rules ranged from lashings to death.

These changes required careful planning and preparation. In 1934 the SS was still relatively small. It took a while for them to turn into the terrifying instrument of power and terror of 1938, just as the Wehrmacht needed time before the officially 100,000-man-strong Reichswehr of 1933—though in fact it probably was somewhat stronger—became the powerful military machine Hitler needed for his war.

Because the perfection of the terror and the military buildup took some time, the years from 1934 to 1938 gave the appearance of comparative stability. The real nature of Hitlerism, which asserted itself more and more after 1938, was put on temporary hold.

The man in charge of Hitler's terror was Heinrich Himmler, the supreme commander of the SS. In that area he was Hitler's right hand. The man in charge of the other building block of Hitler's state—propaganda—was Joseph Goebbels, the inventor of a new department of government, the Reich Ministry for Enlightenment and Propaganda. He has been called Hitler's invaluable left hand.

Goebbels never held the same sort of semi-independent position of power Himmler carved out for himself in the course of time. He remained an executor, a functionary, and unlike Himmler he never played any role in policymaking, foreign or domestic. Still, Goebbels oversaw one of the most important states within Hitler's state. He had complete control over what nowadays is referred to as the public media, over all areas with the potential of influencing and shaping public opinion, above all the press and broadcasting, but also the stage, film, and to some degree publishing as well. Goebbels was a master of communication techniques.

Goebbels never tried to turn all Germans into National Socialists. All he did was use the media, and film in particular, to offer a view of a society whose health had been restored under the Führer, under National Socialism. His ministry made occasional propaganda films, but their number can be counted on the fingers of one hand. The films he sponsored were humorous, lighthearted, polished entertainments in which love conquered all and no one said "Heil Hitler" or mentioned the Third Reich. These movies gave the German people what they were looking for—escape.

Oddly enough, much of Goebbels's propaganda was made with the help of people who thought of themselves as anti-Nazis. Most of the working actors and directors were so-called Antis. By making pictures that more or less ignored the Third Reich, they managed to convince themselves that they were resisting. What they failed to see was that in making these seemingly harmless confections devoid of any hint of Nazi propaganda, they were doing Goebbels's bidding and helping to cover over the reality. They were saying that things were only half as bad, that all in all life was really quite normal. I am not pointing a finger. Like anybody else, they had to make a living, and anyone who was making a living in the Third Reich was in one way or another helping it. My point is that for them to claim now that by not making propaganda they were part of a resistance movement, as some actors have implied, is not quite accurate.

Goebbels's press policy was not very different. He did not ban the non-Socialist papers, only those of the Social Democratic and Communist press. All the others were allowed to continue. Nor can it be said that Goebbels actually Nazified them. Of course, Nazi journalists were put into editorial offices, as watchdogs, so to speak, but as a rule they did not hold key positions. Most of the editorial staffs of the major non-Socialist papers were kept on—except for Jewish journalists, of course. And those who stayed on were expected to carry on as usual. The press of the Third Reich was still diverse. The readers of Frankfurt's major daily were not handed the same diet as those of the official Nazi daily, and even that paper was not like the *Stürmer*, the official organ of the mono-maniacal anti-Semite Streicher. The reader was given a choice; the news was made palatable.

Goebbels's intervention was unobtrusive. The daily press briefings of the Propaganda Ministry were conducted by a subordinate, rarely by Goebbels himself. The papers usually sent a correspondent rather than the top editor to these briefings. The purpose of these sessions was to give so-called language guidance, not detailed directives or instructions. The papers were allowed, and even encouraged, to continue in their traditional style. The purpose of the directive was to let them know what not to emphasize or what to gloss over and what to feature prominently. In some rare instances they were told what editorial line to take. It would therefore be unfair to say that the press was completely coordinated. It remained diverse, but limits to what could be printed were set. Goebbels and Hitler achieved their objective of letting the non-Nazis know what they wanted them to hear in a way they could accept. By not overwhelming the public with ideas they felt it was not yet ready for, they succeeded brilliantly in manipulating public opinion and the public mood. Moreover, the propaganda machinery had a comparatively easy time between 1934 and 1938 because things were going well for Hitler. Even the non-Nazis were forced to concede that not only did Hitler *know* what he wanted, he also *did* what he wanted. After all, they said, just look at him. Let him be, he's making us rich and great and strong. He's showing the world that Germany again is a force to be reckoned with.

In those years Hitler scored three major victories. The first was full employment. Employment also was under the aegis of a state within the state, not under Hitler's personal auspices. It was largely the domain of Hjalmar Schacht, a former Democratic party politician. At first he was head of the State Bank, and later he became the chief of Hitler's Economic Ministry. Schacht stimulated the economy through rigidly compartmentalized domestic economic measures— through credits without immediately felt inflationary consequences. The years from 1936 to 1939 were a time of unimagined well-being in which both sides, business and labor, were prospering—very different from the crisis days of Brüning. One must not underestimate the effects of the economy on the political climate. In those Hitler years the weather was benign.

The second big success Hitler scored in those years was his decision to rearm. It helped him overcome any misgivings the Reichswehr might still have harbored. Nor should one underestimate the professional and personal benefits rearmament brought to the officers' corps of the old Reichswehr. In the new big army promotions proliferated: lieutenants became colonels, colonels generals, generals field marshals. In short, everybody was doing well, not only materially but professionally. They were finally again allowed to show what they could do; they were part of an expanding military apparatus. Under these circumstances it would be foolish to go into opposition; it was easier to swallow all sorts of distasteful decrees, such as the introduction of the Aryan Paragraph in 1935. Of course, the Reichswehr had never had all that many Jewish officers to begin with, but it did have quite a number with a Jewish grandparent, for intermarriage between the military aristocracy and the Jewish finance aristocracy had not been all that rare. The unfortunate offspring of these unions were now forced to leave the Reichswehr. This caused some ripples and some bad feeling, but it was accepted. What mattered most was that the army was becoming strong, a powerful weapon, just as in the good old days of the kaiser.

Hitler's third success, which Goebbels's skilled salesmanship also impressed on the German people, was his defiant foreign policy, very different from that of Stresemann and the republic's. Although these governments had also been revisionist, and successfully so, they had stressed accommodation and conciliation. Not so Hitler. His method was success through defiance.

He had started out on that road in 1933, when Germany demonstratively slammed the door on the League of Nations, which it had joined only seven years earlier. Hitler very skillfully made his disaffiliation the occasion for his first plebiscite, which he won almost unanimously. Then in 1935 came the reintroduction of universal military service, his avowal that Germany would expand its standing army to thirty-six divisions—not a word about the Versailles Treaty and its 100,000-man limit on the army—and his proclaimed intention to resurrect Germany's air arm. And in 1936 he made his boldest move, by which Germany scuttled not only the Versailles Treaty but also the voluntarily signed Locarno Pact of 1925: The Wehrmacht moved into the demilitarized zone of the Rhineland. This led to the first crisis of Hitler's pre-1938 foreign policy. For a moment it seemed that France would confront him by mobilizing and sending its armies into the Rhineland. A number of Reichswehr generals, fearing such a French response, opposed Hitler's move, but he gambled that France would not act, and he proved to be right. The people began to feel that from now on Germany could do whatever it wanted, that nobody would dare bar its way. And with this defiance he probably scored the most significant of all his domestic psychological victories.

After this came the truly big, unanticipated successes of 1938: the unopposed peaceful march into Austria and the *Anschluss*, one of the goals of the earlier revisionists. In the fall of 1938— albeit after the first real threat of a crisis—came the Munich Pact in which France and England sold out Czechoslovakia, France's ally, and forced the Czechs to cede the Sudetenland, a predominantly ethnic German border region, to Germany.

The feeling throughout Germany was that Hitler had the Midas touch, that he was God's gift to them, that he had given them more than they had dared hope for. It no longer mattered that other parts of his program were never completely popular.

What about these other parts? From the very beginning Hitler had relentlessly persecuted two groups: the Communists and the Jews. In view of the fact that by 1932 the Communists had become a mass party and got six million votes, one might have thought that his anti-Communist campaign would not be all that popular. One may well ask what happened to those six million votes after 1933. The answer is, nothing.

Even the non-Socialist and Socialist adversaries of the Communists had secretly hoped that the Communists would be able to mount some sort of resistance against Hitler (something they themselves were no longer ready to undertake), that the Communists would not let themselves be wiped out by Hitler without a struggle. There even was fear of something like a civil war breaking out. However, nothing like that ever happened. After the Reichstag fire the Communist leaders who had not fled the country or gone underground were arrested and sent to concentration camps. The party offices were searched and closed, and the staffs arrested. The Communist party was in effect made illegal without an official ban. The tactic was a complete success; there was no Communist resistance worth mentioning.

A great many Communist voters and supporters, probably a few million, deserted the party in the following months. The non-Socialist parties, and to some degree also the Social Democrats who had waged a fraternal battle against the Communists, were not altogether unhappy with what was happening to them. It must be pointed out, however, that while the non-Socialist parties disappeared without a trace, and while the SPD had gone into exile, Communists inside Germany continued to risk their lives to maintain at least some cadres, some link between the most important party outposts. That sort of perseverance against all odds is more than admirable, although it must also be admitted that in all that time they accomplished nothing. Small Communist groups and grouplets formed and re-formed, and at times even managed to carry out some minor campaigns, like leaving leaflets in public buildings. The only thing they accomplished, however, was to create martyrs. At any rate, Hitler's anti-Communism had no adverse effect, neither on the ready acceptance of his policies nor on his enormous popularity.

Anti-Semitism was a different matter. Neither the German Reich of the Hohenzollern nor the Prussia of Hardenberg and Bismarck had been anti-Semitic states. The anti-Semitism of the German people was at most "conventional"; in the provinces Jews were not always liked and often socially isolated. There was some resentment against their attraction to certain professions (law, medicine, journalism, publishing, literature), but it was a social, nonviolent anti-Semitism. And it was not shared by the majority of the people.

Popular attitudes toward the Jews fell into three categories. First there was the one that approved of Jewish emancipation and equality under the law, in line with Hardenberg's dictum of 1911: "Equal rights, equal duties." The second differentiated between converts and nonconverts, or between old residents and newcomers. The former were accepted and the latter were kept at arm's length. And then there were the rabid anti-Semites who would have liked to deprive the Jews, or at least all nonconverts and recent arrivals, of their civil rights. The extremists among these even wanted to deprive Jews of their citizenship. But none, not even the most vehement, ever advocated the extermination of the Jews. This idea, part and parcel of Hitler's ideology which he ultimately turned into horrible reality, had never even been hinted at in pre-Hitler Germany.

Hitler led up to this part of his program step by step. First he merely closed certain positions and professions to Jews, and even then veterans and the children of war heroes were exempted. Then the proscription was extended to more and more professions, after which he took the first truly momentous step: the proclamation of the Nuremberg Laws of 1935, which deprived Jews of all civil rights and forbade intermarriage and sexual relationships between Jews and non-Jews. This was a significant and not particularly popular move. Still it was accepted, probably also because it institutionalized the most radical proposals of the rabid anti-Semites; as a result, many people chose to believe that with this Hitler's anti-Semitic campaign had reached its acme. Henceforth, so they told themselves, the Jews would know where they stood. True, they no longer had any civil rights, some professions were closed to them, they could no longer marry Gentiles or have affairs with them, and, well, perhaps this was going a bit far, but compared to all the good things Hitler was doing—jobs, rearmament, foreign-policy successes, the restoration of Germany's self-esteem—one could live with the Nuremberg Laws.

This acquiescence in the persecution of the Jews ultimately led to the acceptance of far more terrible things, and with it the German people also became guilty of Hitler's crimes against the Jews, even though after the obliteration of all democratic political channels they no longer were able to voice their objections or give them political force.

On a personal level it was possible to oppose Hitler's anti-Jewish laws. Even if Germans could no longer marry Jews, they could risk punishment and live with Jews. Later, once the persecutions began in earnest, one could hide Jews or help them escape or assist them in some other way. And many people did just that; not millions perhaps, but thousands at any rate. It was no longer possible, however, even if one wanted to, effectively to fight specific aspects of Hitler's rule, such as his anti-Semitic regulations. Still, Hitler's anti-Semitism was the line that separated the loyal followers of the Führer—the majority of the people—and the not insignificant minority of Antis, people who in the privacy of their homes railed against Hitler and his party, and who were convinced that this proved their adherence to traditional values even if they no longer dared to speak out, let alone act. There always existed a substantial number of Antis who later, after Hitler's fall, liked to describe themselves as the "inner emigration," or even as the resistance. I believe that both these labels should be used with great caution.

Resistance was limited to very small groups, and occasionally to groups that were officially part of the regime, particularly in the military; outside the official apparatus no effective resistance was possible. The resistance of some of the churches and of the Communists was ineffective because neither was in any position to affect the policies of the Führer state. In fact, there was only *one* group that had the necessary leverage: the General Staff of the army. There were two officers' plots, one in 1938–39, when war was imminent, and the other in 1943–44, when defeat was imminent. Only one of these plots was actually carried out: Count Stauffenberg's botched assassination of Hitler on July 20, 1944. Stauffenberg failed largely because he did not have the backing of the entire army command, only of a minority. Of this minority only a few escaped Hitler's vengeance. They deserve respect, but they too accomplished nothing.

The "internal emigration" is another matter. There was of course an actual emigration, but emigration was not all that simple. The world was in the grip of economic crisis, and very few countries were ready to admit immigrants and allow them to work. Many Germans undoubtedly would have liked to withdraw into an inner emigration, but strangely enough that was not possible. Let me cite the example of Heinrich Lübke, the future president of the Federal Republic.

Lübke, a former leader of the Center party, had not capitulated to the Nazis in 1933, and consequently a political career was closed to him. He decided to fall back on his original profession, civil engineering, a completely nonpolitical vocation. Perhaps this may be seen as an act of inner emigration. By trading in his promising political career for an anonymous middle-class position, Lübke voluntarily accepted the loss of prestige as the price for living up to his beliefs. But can this really be called an act of inner emigration? As a civil engineer he had to work for the Reich, for example to help build camps for slave laborers, which was one of the (I believe unfair) charges later leveled against him. At any rate, Lübke has more right to consider himself part of the inner emigration than many an Anti who helped Goebbels carry out his program in the press, radio, theater, or literature.

Let me get back to literature, because it was the least controlled medium. Many prominent German writers had emigrated. Still, in the Third Reich books continued to be written by Antis who circumvented official controls by writing romantic trifles, adventure stories, and similar confections. Their readers knew that these authors wished to distance themselves from the Nazis. But might it not be said that they, by showing that such an escape hatch existed, were actually playing the game? Everyone who worked under Goebbels, regardless of any self-bestowed anti-Nazi credentials, played an instrument in Goebbels' orchestra. All those romances, those old-fashioned tales, everything that was part of so-called normal life, without directly challenging the Third Reich, was part of the grand scheme.

I would like to close this chapter with a frequently asked yet still unanswered and unresolved question: Did the Third Reich represent continuity in the history of the German Reich or did it depart from the beaten path? The simple answer is that it contained elements of both continuity and discontinuity, and that continuity predominated. As we shall see, Hitler adopted the "world power or collapse" alternative of the late Wilhelmine Empire and of World War I, and in that respect his foreign policy fell completely within a continuity that had been forcibly interrupted by the lost war.

Hitler's domestic policy, the actual constitution of his Reich, is another matter. At first glance it appears to represent utter discontinuity, for there was no precedent for one-man dictatorship or state terror, for the propaganda monopoly or the dismantling of all political parties. However, strange as this may seem, all these innovations were readily accepted in 1933, as though everyone had been waiting for them all along. These were indeed unprecedented measures, yet perhaps something in the background of the German Reich had paved the way for them. Bismarck was no dictator, yet in his early years he had molded the policy of "his" Reich as autocratically as Hitler shaped his in its final phase. The legacy he left, intentionally or not, was a conscious or subconscious yearning for a leader. And the same holds true for the people's distaste for political parties. In the second half of World War I as well as in the closing days of the Weimar Republic, both these sentiments rose to the surface, and both times Hindenburg was the central figure symbolizing these tendencies. But Hindenburg never translated these dreams into reality, neither between 1916 and 1918 nor between 1930 and 1932. Hitler, on the other hand, acted promptly in 1933, and for years afterward even outdid all the nationalist hopes for national community (and unity) and national grandeur—the ultimate and highest, almost religious aspiration. Hitler's "You are nothing, the *Volk* is everything" had always been the secret ingredient of the political ideology and aspirations of almost all early national movements, and of the citizens of the German Reich. In that respect Hitler stands well within the continuity of German history, even if his methods put everything known or tried in the past into the shade.

Society in Hitler's Reich underwent a change, but in the final analysis continuity predominated. One might say continuity underwent a change. Politically the old ruling class was more or less stripped of power, but it retained its social status. The big landowners remained big landowners, the big industrialists remained big industrialists, and the intellectual and cultural elite, insofar as emigration had not thinned its ranks, also retained its position. What changed was the expansion of these ruling elites, for example the infiltration of the police by the SS, the infiltration of major economic enterprises by Nazi bigwigs, and the changes in press empires, many of which had been in Jewish hands. Society in the time of Hitler was upwardly mobile, as was also true, in a different sense, of the Weimar Republic, and as is still true of the two new German states. That does not mean that continuity had ended. The military's recapture of the social prestige and status it had temporarily forfeited in the Weimar Republic is part of this continuity.

The major element of discontinuity was Hitler's anti-Semitism, the biological race theory, a theory without credence in the former Reich, yet one to which Hitler may have attached even greater importance than to his actual leadership role. For the majority of Germans, insofar as they were neither Jews nor had close links to Jews, this remained a minor issue; they could ignore or accept it as long as the Reich remained as unified and powerful as it had become. And that feeling did not change until the end. I am anticipating the end because the persecution and extermination of the Jews does not belong in the next chapter, which deals with the history of World War II. The mass murder of the Jews was not an act of war, even though it took place during the war.

After 1938 the anti-Jewish campaign grew more virulent. In that year Hitler decided to test the public mood and the effect of his anti-Semitic propaganda by launching a nationwide pogrom. For this purpose he once again called on the practically impotent SA. The test results were negative.

The fairly harmless designation *Kristallnacht* is indicative of the German people's response to this pogrom. The events responsible for this comparatively innocuous name were the least of what took place that day. Shop windows were not the only things that were smashed: Jewish homes were razed, synagogues were torched, thousands of Jews were arrested and shipped to concentration camps, and some were killed. That was not a crystal-smashing night, it was a pogrom. The people refused to acknowledge it. They distanced themselves, they did not take part; there even were some public displays of disgust. At the same time, they sought to minimize the horror of it all by tagging it *Kristallnacht*, a nasty yet semicomical excess for which they disclaimed all responsibility. Yet at the same time they did not wish to hold National Socialism itself responsible, and most certainly not the Führer.

Be that as it may, from Hitler's vantage point the test did not live up to expectations, and he called a halt after twenty-four hours. He had found out that the mass of German people, his faithful and obedient minions, were not ready to take an active part in anti-Jewish excesses. Hitler learned a lesson from this, one that is often overlooked. When he embarked on the Final Solution, he did not carry it out on German soil. The extermination camps were put into eastern Poland. Germany itself, and various other countries, were the scenes of Jewish "transports": the removal of Jews, allegedly for resettlement in other areas. Unlike the other extreme acts and crimes of the Third Reich, the mass murder, the systematic extermination of millions of Jews, was never publicized, let alone trumpeted. Goebbels's superb propaganda machinery was not activated. The German press under Goebbels's control never said that the Jews must be exterminated, and certainly not that they were actually *being* exterminated. Even as late as 1945 they kept on playing the same old tune about the Jews being Germany's misfortune who must not be trusted. As far as the German newspaper readers and radio listeners were concerned, there was no Holocaust.

This conscious hiding of the Holocaust from the German public partially explains their failure to act. Another, and I believe even more valid, explanation is the fact that even if they had known they could not have done anything about it under the conditions that prevailed in the second half of the war.

Whether or not the Germans knew about the mass murder of the Jews is a question that can be answered only on an individual basis. Of course a great deal seeped through. Was it believed? I don't know. For a long time it also was not believed outside of Germany; the horror of it all went beyond the limits of the human imagination. The German Jews themselves did not believe that anything of this kind could happen, or more of them might have tried to flee after 1938.

A history of the German Reich cannot ignore the persecution of the Jews and their programmatic extermination. It happened, and it is an ineradicable blot on the history of Germany. Yet on the other hand, it cannot be put into the same category as other aspects of that history which, like so much else in the Führer state, were rooted in the history and nature of the German Reich. After 1933 something like a Führer state would probably have come into being even without Hitler. And there probably would have been another war even without Hitler. But not the murder of millions of Jews.

9

World War II

THE WAR HITLER IGNITED on September 1, 1939, was not the war he had visualized and planned. The lesson he had learned from World War I was that the war in the East against Russia had been won by Germany. Because Russia turned out to be weaker than anticipated, it was forced to sign a dictated peace, and so by the end of the war a great deal of Russian land ended up in German hands. Hitler was convinced that he would be able to duplicate this outcome.

As he wrote in *Mein Kampf*: "It seems as though fate itself wanted to point the way. The vast Eastern empire is on the verge of collapse."

Hitler also recognized that England was largely responsible for Germany's defeat in the West and that the war against England might perhaps have been avoided. There were many similarities between the events leading up to World War War I and those leading up to World War II. Bethmann Hollweg had been eager to keep England neutral in the event of a continental war against France and Russia, a war he believed was sure to come, and Hitler too made every effort to keep England neutral, or better still to have England on his side. He also thought he knew the reason for the earlier failure to keep England neutral: because Germany, although hemmed in on the continent by France and Russia, persisted in beefing up its fleet. This had needlessly challenged England to a contest over hegemony outside Europe. Hitler wisely decided not to make the same mistake: no fleet buildup, no world politics, but, rather, concentration on the war against Russia, possibly after a short war against France to protect the rear. It is remarkable, and probably no accident, that this logical plan, so carefully worked out between 1933 and 1938, failed.

In 1935 Hitler signed a naval pact with England in which he agreed to limit the German fleet to a third of Britain's, which was not all that painful a concession considering that Germany had practically no fleet to speak of. But perhaps Hitler signed this agreement in good faith. He did not want a war with England or to challenge England. He wanted England to stand by and watch Germany conquer Bolshevik Russia and make it into a German sphere of influence. Hitler sent Ribbentrop on a mission to London with instructions to come back with a signed agreement.

England, however, did not want any agreement with Germany, nor was it ready to accede to Germany's conquest and subjugation of Russia. But it was willing to make major concessions if Germany would accept the status quo on the continent, that is, if Germany agreed to spare France and leave Russia alone.

The basic issue in the German-English negotiations of 1937 and 1939 was Germany's war against Russia. England sought to prevent such a war, not out of affection for the Soviet Union— on the contrary, Russian-British relations were quite bad—but because it realized that a German conquest of the Soviet Union would make Germany, even without a strong navy, far more powerful than England and France. England hoped to dissuade Germany from its projected war of conquest in the East and refused to give Germany the free hand in the East that Ribbentrop openly demanded in Hitler's name. England's response to Ribbentrop's proposal was a policy that came to be known as appeasement.

England proposed to use its influence to help

Germany win major concessions, including control over the German-speaking regions Hitler wanted to integrate into the Reich: Austria, the border regions of Czechoslovakia, and probably Danzig as well. In return, Germany was to commit itself to working together with England and France, particularly with England, to preserve the peace in Europe.

Thus between 1937 and 1939 two conflicting concepts met head-on: Hitler's, which visualized a benevolently neutral England standing by and watching Germany's conquest of the East, and Britain's, which hoped that a satiated, appeased Germany would become part of a peaceful Europe.

England's motives were not purely altruistic. Peace was of overriding importance to England. In case of a European war, England was sure to be drawn in. That would expose the fragility of Britain's worldwide colonial empire—in eastern Asia, in the Mediterranean, in the Near East—for England did not feel strong enough to defend its overseas empire against the other two aggressive revisionist powers, Japan and Italy.

One of the most interesting aspects of this diplomatic balancing act between Germany and England was the fact that initially only Germany stood to gain from it, for it would have allowed Germany to expand and regain its power position on the continent. With the help of the Western powers Hitler could have realized the Central European concept of World War I and averted a second world war. However, that was not enough for him.

The first head-on clash in the contest between these two opposing concepts was the Sudeten crisis of 1938; at issue were the ethnic-German border regions of Czechoslovakia. It is generally assumed that this crisis ended in a complete and uncontested victory for Hitler. Even though England and France had been instrumental in the creation of Czechoslovakia after World War I, and even though France still had a pact with Czechoslovakia, the Western powers narrowly averted war by handing over the Sudetenland to Hitler at a hurriedly convened summit meeting at Munich.

To repeat: This looked like Hitler's greatest triumph. And after Munich the military's opposition to Hitler, which had resurfaced during this crisis, collapsed completely. Yet strangely enough Hitler did not see the prize he won at Munich as a victory; he would have preferred a quick war against Czechoslovakia. What triumphed in Munich was not so much Hitler's planning as Britain's policy of appeasement. When the British Prime Minister Neville Chamberlain returned to London from Munich, he proclaimed that the conference had brought "peace in our time."

The English undoubtedly figured that the countries of southeastern Europe would seek an accommodation with Hitler, and that Hitler would need anywhere from five to ten years to organize the spheres of interest more or less handed to him on a platter. During that time, they reasoned, Hitler would not be able to plan any major campaigns, leaving the West time to rearm in peace and reestablish military parity with Germany. But Hitler did not take the time. He adhered to his Russian plan, convinced that he could execute it without England, and if necessary even against England. After Munich he tended to be somewhat contemptuous of England. That brought him to the crisis of 1939.

All in all, 1939 began rather calmly. In England there was the feeling that appeasement had worked. But Hitler was not interested in organizing eastern and southeastern Central Europe under German aegis. If he had any plans at all for that region it was to win the support of some of the neighboring countries for his planned war against Russia, and he focused his sights on the Poles.

Poland, being situated between Germany and Russia, threatened to obstruct Hitler's plans. For how could he launch a war against Russia in the absence of a joint German-Russian military border somewhere along the line? From the German perspective that border ideally ought to be as far to the east as possible. In other words, it seemed advisable to recruit Poland for the campaign against Russia. In return, if Poland agreed to conclude a twenty-five-year pact with Germany, to cede Danzig to Germany, and to pledge its active cooperation in a future German war against the Soviet

Union, Germany was ready to give Poland a part of the Ukraine.

Poland refused, and it was this refusal rather than the question of Danzig that led Hitler to change his plans. If Poland could not be induced to enter into an agreement with him, then he would simply have to overrun and occupy it. The planned war against Russia would have to be put off until after the war against Poland—a war that threatened to involve him in a war against England as well, for in the meantime Hitler's actions had also brought about a change in England's position.

In addition to giving Hitler the Sudetenland, the agreement reached at Munich also stipulated—and from the British perspective this was probably the most important provision—that Germany would not undertake any foreign ventures without prior consultation with England. That rankled Hitler. He wanted a free hand in the East. And so, defying England, he decided to occupy rump Czechoslovakia and divide it up without prior notice to England. Bohemia-Moravia became a "Reich protectorate," and Slovakia a vassal state. It was a gratuitous provocation, because rump Czechoslovakia was putty in Hitler's hands anyway. It seems Hitler was avenging Munich, or at least that portion of the agreement he felt to be a defeat for himself and a victory for England.

The move into Czechoslovakia in March 1939 alarmed England. The Chamberlain government still did not give up on the policy of appeasement, but it changed its methods. Up to then they had tried to lure Hitler with promises and concessions; now they also resorted to threats. If Hitler continued his autocratic eastward expansion, he was told, he would find England blocking his way. To underscore this threat, Britain at the end of March 1939, after Poland turned down Hitler's invitation to join him in an anti-Russian alliance, announced that it would help preserve Poland's independence.

Britain's guarantee changed the picture. Hitler himself summed it up in his message of August 11, 1939, three weeks before the outbreak of the war, when he told Karl J. Burckhardt, the League of Nations commissar in Danzig: "Everything I do is directed against Russia. If the West is too stupid and too blind to see this I shall be forced to reach an understanding with Russia and fight the West, and then, once the West is defeated, turn against the Soviet Union with all the power at my command."

These words hold the key for the outbreak of World War II. This was Hitler's new improvised program, and it was the plan he followed in the first two years of the war. Hitler made an agreement with the Soviet Union, and together with the Soviet Union he turned against Poland; then, with the Soviet Union covering his rear, he turned against the West. Only after that, as promised, did he turn against the Soviet Union "with all the power at [his] command."

But why did the Soviet Union go along with this plan? Stalin must have been aware of Hitler's ultimate designs on the Soviet Union, and Hitler did nothing to make him think otherwise. Since 1936 he had concluded a series of anti-Comintern pacts with a number of countries—Japan, Italy, and also some smaller ones. These pacts were actually anti-Soviet alliances with secret clauses pledging neutrality in case of a German war against the Soviet Union.

In 1939 Stalin saw a chance for averting such a war by tossing the ball to the West. He thought to keep Hitler from going to war against the Soviet Union for as long as possible by involving Germany in a war with England and France. Under these circumstances Stalin was more than willing to make an arrangement with Hitler to divide East Europe between the Soviet Union and Germany.

On August 23, 1939, Germany and the Soviet Union concluded a nonaggression pact. It contained secret provisions to the effect that in case of a war against Poland, the Soviet Union would get back the parts of eastern Poland it had ceded to Poland in 1921, and furthermore that it would be given control over the Baltic border states and Finland. Similar and somewhat vague conditions were also agreed upon with regard to southeast Europe.

That is how the war ignited by Hitler began on September 1, 1939. A war with Poland, and consequently also with France and England, and with the Soviet Union as his ally, was not the war Hitler had had in mind; it was the war General Seeckt and the Reichswehr had had in mind in the twenties. As mentioned earlier, Hitler saw it as the prelude to the big war against the Soviet Union, which he was going to wage with all his might once Poland and the West had been defeated.

That, however, was not to be. At first things went very well for Hitler. After a surprisingly brief campaign Poland was smashed in September 1939, and after some time during which negotiations continued and Germany occupied Denmark and Norway, France was defeated in June 1940, in a war that lasted all of six weeks. In the course of this Western campaign Holland, Belgium, and Luxembourg were also attacked, overrun, and occupied.

Once Poland and France were knocked out of the war, the question facing Hitler was how to proceed with regard to England. The German Reich was not as well prepared for an invasion, conquest, and occupation of England as it had been for the war against Poland and France. It was still without a big navy; moreover, it had lost part of its fleet in its Norwegian campaign. The only chance for Hitler to land his army on the British Isles was to gain control of the air.

He tried to do this in August and September 1940, but he failed. England retained control over its air space, and that meant that a German invasion of England was not in the cards for the foreseeable future. Whether it could still have succeeded even under optimum conditions as late as 1942 or 1943 is questionable; in the interim England had grown stronger on land as well.

The significance of the defeat of the German air arm in the battle of Britain has been underestimated. The air war itself was not a particularly dramatic development; it was not a catastrophe on the order of, say, Stalingrad two years later. However, it did mark a turning point, because it showed that Hitler's victory in the West was incomplete. If Hitler nonetheless planned to go ahead with his war against Russia, he could no longer do it "with all the power at [his] command." A very tough, resourceful enemy was blocking the way in the West, and moreover one with close ties to the United States.

For a while Hitler made halfhearted efforts to knock England out of the war, with air raids over London and other English cities through the winter of 1940 into the following spring. That strategy was as unavailing as the later, far bigger British-American air offensive over Germany, another strategic miscalculation.

Hitler continued to be weighed down by the war against England, and the question arose whether under these circumstances he could afford a war against Russia. After much to and fro and many heated discussions, not to mention a time-consuming involvement in the war between

Italy and England that had meanwhile erupted, he decided that he could risk it. In June 1941 he did what he had promised in August 1939: Even though England was still in the war, he attacked Russia, if not with all the strength at his command, still with his massive land and air power.

In retrospect, one can say that this was Hitler's first major strategic blunder in this war, and that it alone was enough to make him lose the war. For despite great initial successes it soon became evident that Russia could not be defeated like Poland and France, that in the face of losses that in all likelihood would have brought any other European nation to its knees, Russia was able to mobilize its entire population and outlast the German Reich.

Hitler did not understand the changes that had taken place in Russia since the twenties. When Hitler wrote in *Mein Kampf* that the huge empire in the East was on the brink of collapse, he may have been right. The young Soviet Union, after the ravages of World War I, the civil war, and the wars of intervention, was a rubble heap, a vast but exhausted, devastated country that most likely would not have been able to defend itself against a German attack.

Since then, however, Russia had come under Stalin's rule, an era of total concentration of all of its energies, during which pre–World War I agrarian Russia was transformed into a substantial industrial power. The Soviet Union Hitler went

to war against in 1941 was not the superpower it is today, but it was an industrial power of considerable weight. Industrialization in conjunction with existing resources—the size of the country, the bravery and resilience of its vast population—made the Soviet Union a far more formidable adversary than the Russia of World War I.

Hitler won major battles and conquered much territory, but his attack faltered at the gates of Leningrad and Moscow and Rostov-on-Don. After months of defeat the Russians in the winter of 1941–42 were still able to launch a fairly successful military counteroffensive.

At the very moment of this Russian counteroffensive, in early December 1941, when it became obvious that Russia was not going to be overcome as quickly as anticipated, when Hitler was clearly facing a long, difficult struggle against the Soviet Union, when victory was by no means certain—at that very moment Hitler decided to declare war on the United States. This must be the most puzzling of any of his decisions in World War II. I cannot explain it. In my writings I have discussed a number of possible reasons and have read the various theories advanced by historians, yet I must admit that none of the explanations, neither my own hypotheses nor those of others, are very enlightening.

To go back: Since President Roosevelt's famous speech of 1937 in which he called for quarantining the aggressor nations—Japan, Italy, and

Germany—there was no dearth of signals concerning Roosevelt's determination to intervene in a war started by any of these countries. But it was also clear that he faced much domestic opposition. Public opinion and the Congress remained isolationist. They wanted no part of the conflicts in the Old World; they were determined not to repeat the error of World War I and become involved in a European War on the side of the Entente.

Before December 1941 Roosevelt was unable to break through this isolationist resistance to his interventionism. There is no way of telling when and whether he would ever have succeeded if Hitler's declaration of war had not come along. Even after the Japanese attack on Pearl Harbor, or rather because of the prospect of a major war in the Pacific, Hitler still had reason to hope that America would not intervene in the European war for some time to come. True, the war in the Pacific enabled America to mobilize its vast resources, but at the same time they were being deployed in the Pacific against Japan, a theater that posed no danger to Germany.

Hitler, however, used the Japanese attack as the occasion to declare war on the United States, almost as though he had lain in wait for just such a moment, and thereby gave Roosevelt what he wanted, a chance to enter the war against Germany on the side of England. Of course, this still took a great deal of time. Not until the summer of 1944 was America militarily strong enough to

invade the continent in concert with England. But once Hitler had done Roosevelt the favor of declaring war on the United States, Germany's defeat could no longer be staved off. Why then did he do it?

Even if this question cannot be answered unequivocally, some thoughts do offer themselves.

In July 1941, after his great initial successes, Hitler thought that the war against Russia was in the bag. At that moment, when the first step toward Germany's defeat had in fact already been taken, Hitler developed plans that went far beyond his original idea of incorporating Russia into the German sphere. That July he decided to cut back his buildup of the army, formerly a priority item because of the planned attack on Russia, in favor of a major naval expansion. As far as Hitler was concerned the war against the Soviet Union had already been won, and he was preparing for a worldwide blitzkrieg in which a big navy and air force would neutralize the United States before it could reach its full strength.

Not only did these grandiose plans never reach fruition, they never even got as far as the projected naval buildup, because beginning in 1942 the war against Russia once more moved to center stage. Still, those plans existed, and perhaps they even lived on in Hitler's head until the end of 1941. In a heedless moment he may even have believed as late as December 1941 that he could still fall back on them, since America seemed to be preoccupied with the Japanese war. However, this is only one of many hypotheses.

One thing is certain: In 1941 Hitler made a fatal error by declaring war on the United States, adding the most powerful country in the world to his circle of enemies while he was still involved in the war against Russia and England. With that he sealed Germany's defeat.

Even after the attack on Poland there was no easy way for Hitler to get out of the war unscathed. Germany perhaps might have, but only under a different government, a government whose word could be trusted, to paraphrase Chamberlain. Obviously Hitler could not be trusted. In 1941 he sealed Germany's fate, first by deciding to take on Russia, and then by declaring war against the United States as well. Nineteen forty-one was the real beginning of World War II; before then it had simply been a limited European war. A direct line led from 1941 to 1945. The outcome was now certain, regardless of what Germany did or did not do.

True, major battles were still fought from 1942 to the end. The United States and England launched a tremendous air offensive against Germany in the hope of avoiding a land war, and they rained death and destruction on Germany. For the population of the occupied territories the final war years were the worst. The people of the Soviet Union suffered more in the long German retreat than they had in the rapid German advance. The

Germans were determined to leave nothing but scorched earth behind. And the world will never forget the horror of the Final Solution, which began in 1941 in the occupied Soviet territory and in 1942 was extended to all of occupied Europe.

There were still moments in 1942 and 1943 when a desperate, suffering Russia appeared willing to let Hitler get out of the war in the East by a cease-fire if he were to withdraw to the old line of demarcation or the old German borders. Hitler never agreed to that—and in effect one can forget about all these conjectures. They never were seriously considered.

The only question that must still be asked about the second half of World War II is why Hitler, in a situation with no prospect of victory and once his enemies, after some bickering, had reached agreement on Germany's unconditional surrender and carried the war into Germany, held out amid the ruins of Berlin until his last-minute suicide—and even managed to find fanatics ready to impose his will on a terrified populace.

Two theories have been advanced. According to one, Hitler never wavered in his belief in final victory. After all, in his own political life he had miraculously bounced back time and again. Perhaps he hoped that the East-West alliance would disintegrate at the very moment of victory, permitting him to make a separate peace with one and defeat the other. There is much to be said for such a scenario. In the winter of 1944–45 he still came back to this, not publicly, but in secret meetings with his generals. He told them that he was like the spider in his web waiting for a falling-out between the West and the Soviet Union. The only thing wrong with this picture was that he was not the spider but the fly. He failed to understand that the disagreements over the postwar order and the ideological differences between the West and the Russians would not surface, let alone lead to an armed clash, as long as a Germany at war with both of them acted as a buffer. Before the possibility of a third world war could arise, Germany had to be defeated and occupied, the two big power blocs had to meet and confront each other in the heart of Germany. Every delay in this process kept the differences between the two blocs from erupting. As long as Germany stayed in the war, their conflict was bound to remain latent. Thus Germany's continued resistance prevented the very thing Hitler hoped for. His calculation about a possible disintegration of the East-West alliance, if indeed there was one, was a miscalculation. We have no proof that Hitler actually continued to believe in final victory up to the very end. His reasons for continuing the war to the last man might have been psychological rather than political.

There was something mock-heroic about Hitler. According to fairly reliable sources, Göring allegedly told him in August 1939, "Let's stop this

gamble," to which Hitler replied, "I've been gam-
bling all my life." Whether or not he actually said
it, it was the truth. He was a man who had to go
for broke. If he could not make Germany into *the*
world power then he was prepared to set off the
greatest conflagration in German history. There
are indications that at the end Hitler consciously
desired that catastrophe.

At the end of 1941, when the first signs that
Germany might be facing defeat appeared, Hitler
reportedly told a foreign diplomat: "If the German
people should no longer be strong enough and determined enough to sacrifice their blood for their
survival then let them perish and be destroyed by
another, greater power. I will shed no tears for the
German people." A truly unique admission from
the lips of a German statesman.

At the end of the war, to the horror of many
of his comrades, Hitler did indeed try to turn Germany's military defeat into the annihilation of the
German people.

There exists a document, the so-called Nero
Directive of March 18 and 19, 1945, in which Hitler ordered all still remaining resources of the
Reich, even those vital to the survival of the population, to be destroyed rather than allow them to
fall into the hands of the enemy. If Hitler could
not be the architect of Germany's greatest victory
then at least he could be the architect of its destruction. This order, which epitomizes Hitler's

mentality, was successfully sabotaged, particularly by Albert Speer, his minister of armaments and war production.

Hitler always tended to think in terms of destruction. He wanted to destroy the Jews, he wanted to destroy the Soviet Union, and now, for historical effect, he was willing to destroy Germany. There is of course no proof for this hypothesis, but various reliable reports tend to support it.

By the summer of 1944 Germany's situation had become absolutely hopeless, yet still it fought on to the bitter end, some say heroically. Germany was literally ground down by the armies and air power of the West and the Soviet Union. At the end, every inch of German soil was under occupation; the German army surrendered unconditionally; the last government, appointed by Hitler shortly before his suicide, was arrested; and on July 5, 1945, the three powers, the United States, the Soviet Union, and the United Kingdom—France joined somewhat later—declared themselves the sovereign rulers of Germany. They previously had reached agreement on their respective zones of occupation. The German Reich was administered by the Allied Control Commission, and it continued in this form for a number of years. It was under the unconditional control of foreign powers, and would inevitably fall apart if the four powers could not reach agreement on their German policy.

The dissolution of the German Reich, its collapse, did not happen in 1945. At the Potsdam Conference the Big Three agreed to treat Germany as an economic entity and even grant it a measure of political sovereignty under their aegis. Because this proposal was never put to the test, there are those who persist in the belief that the German Reich still exists. After 1945, however, a great deal changed, and these changes cannot be ignored. Upon closer scrutiny it becomes clear that in fact the German Reich has ceased to exist.

10

The German Reich
after the War

I<small>N</small> 1973 <small>THE</small> S<small>UPREME</small>
Court of the Federal Republic advanced the thesis
that the German Reich still existed, that even
though it lacked legal competence it was a subject
of international law. In 1945 this may still have
been a defensible thesis, but since then events
have invalidated it. I do not think that anybody
today can seriously maintain that the German
Reich still exists in any form whatsoever, even as
an abstraction.

True, in 1945 the German Reich was under the jurisdiction of the four victorious powers, yet in a way it still existed as the object of that jurisdiction. Essentially, what happened in 1945 was to change the German Reich from a subject of political life into its object. It was the Wehrmacht, not the government, that had surrendered unconditionally. An unconditional surrender on the part of Germany itself, a formal handing over of power by the government to the three and later four victors, had never taken place because of a technical error, as it were.

Nonetheless, governmental power was handed over to the Allies, even though not quite as planned. It happened on May 23, 1945, when the rump government of Admiral Dönitz was arrested, and later, on June 5, when the victors unilaterally took over Germany's governmental powers. After that the German Reich existed as their object, as a four-power Reich under foreign control. The continued existence of that Reich, however, depended on the victors' adherence to their original plan of governing and administering the country as a unit, and that did not happen. As was to be expected, the only thing that had held the anti-Hitler alliance together was the fight against Hitler. Once Hitler was defeated, it took only three years for the alliance to fall apart. Still, some of the innovative measures taken during those three years have survived to this day. For example, the West and East zones were subdivided into *Länder* (provinces), and in the West some new provinces even came into being: Northrhine-Westphalia, Lower Saxony, Schleswig-Holstein. Apparently the victors' original intention was that these *Länder* eventually would form a more-or-less loose federation or confederation, a sort of German League. With some modifications these new provinces still exist in southwestern and western Germany. They are part of the Federal Republic. The German Democratic Republic no longer has any *Länder*.

The present-day political parties also date back to the four-power Reich. At the time each of the four zones had four political parties: Communists, Social Democrats, Liberal Democrats, and Christian Democrats. Apparently the victors also thought of these parties as the political base of the future Germany, whatever its form.

The four parties still exist in the Federal Republic, although the Communists were briefly banned and today are only a marginal group. There is no Social Democratic party in the German Democratic Republic, which is controlled by the Communists. Other parties exist, but they have no voice. They are completely dependent on the Communists even though they sit in the People's Chamber as independent organizations.

Other than that, not much is left of the four-power Reich. History did not come to a stop in the three or four immediate postwar years when the label "four-power Reich" still had some meaning. The postwar history of the German Reich is dotted with events that continued to whittle away at the essence of the Reich, until at the end nothing was left of it. I am referring to the years 1949, 1955, 1961, 1971–72, and finally, though some may find this surprising, 1975.

What happened in 1949? In my opinion, the German Reich underwent the greatest changes of all the postwar years. This was the year in which the two new German states, the German Federal Republic in the west and the German Democratic Republic in the east, the former Soviet zone of occupation, came into being.

The founding of the Federal Republic was not free of problems. The minister presidents of the West German *Länder* hesitated about convening the parliamentary council that was to draw up the new constitution—the present Basic Law of the Federal Republic. They were reluctant because they thought, and as it turned out rightly so, that this step would result in the creation of an East German state. They voiced their misgivings in the Preamble to the Basic Law to document their objections for the benefit of posterity. They really did not want a West German state. What they wanted was a unified German state, the German Reich, even if within the limited borders of 1945, and they said so in somewhat circuitous fashion by asserting that they were speaking also for those who were prevented from participating. They called on all Germans to fight for unity and freedom.

This declaration of conscience led the Federal Supreme Court to conclude that the Preamble was a call for reunification and that it established the continuity of the German Reich. Both these interpretations, it seems to me, go beyond what the Preamble actually says. Nowhere does it state that all future governments of the Federal Republic are obligated to work toward German reunification. If the authors of the Basic Law had wanted to say so they would have. The Preamble makes only a vague appeal for the German *people* to "complete" their unity and freedom. Nor does it say that the German Reich still exists, despite what we are now asked to do. If that is what they had wanted to say they also would have said so. On the contrary. The Preamble, in a way, says that the Reich *no longer* exists, since it is to be "completed," recreated, by the German people at some indeterminate future date.

And even in this context there is no mention of the German Reich, only a resolve that German unity is to be regained in freedom. There is no mention of the form of state. To interpret this as referring to the old German Reich in my opinion goes beyond what the Preamble actually says. Yet this interpretation continues to haunt German domestic policy. Regardless of the merits of the argument, there is no denying that the founders of the Federal Republic were creating a new state in West Germany.

The Federal Republic is a new state. It is not a geographic reconstruction of the German Reich nor is it a fragmentary remnant of that Reich. It emerged out of provinces that in part had never existed before. It was formed by parties—the most powerful of them the CDU/CSU (Christian Democratic Union/Christian Social Union)—that had not existed in the German Reich. And the constitution of the Federal Republic is not modeled on any of the constitutions of the German Reich, including Weimar. It is a completely new law. The state that came into being in the West is indeed a new state, and so is the state that sprang up in the Soviet Zone. From the day of its birth this new state had no similarity to any of the previous forms of the German Reich, nor does it claim to be a continuation of the German Reich.

This, however, did not prevent either of these new states from subjectively considering or proclaiming themselves the nucleus of a future, more comprehensive German national state. The GDR maintained that the Federal Republic was a splinter state, and the Federal Republic in turn averred that its greater freedom would act as a magnet for the population of the GDR and thereby bring about a sort of reunification. At the time that was not an entirely unrealistic supposition; there was a substantial westward movement from the Democratic to the Federal Republic. Between 1949 and 1961, millions of people fled from East Germany—without, however, affecting East Germany's survival as a state.

There was another period in which reunification resurfaced as a political issue. In March 1952 Stalin indicated that he stood ready to nullify the agreement by which the two states had been formed. He proposed the reunification of Germany in free elections up to the Oder-Neisse Line, a peace treaty for the new all-German government, and its own army. Furthermore, he proposed the withdrawal of all occupation forces within a year, and—most important of all—a commitment by the victors not to seek any alliances with Germany, and a like commitment by Germany not to enter into any agreements with the victors. The offer was reunification for neutralization.

Stalin's proposal continued to be discussed for three years, and once, in Berlin in 1954, was debated by the foreign ministers of the four powers. The West, particularly the United States, was very suspicious of the offer, and interestingly enough the government of the Federal Republic also tended to play it down. There was some nationalistic opposition to the position of the Adenauer government, particularly in the public media, but it was rather feeble. Occasional voices were raised, the Social Democrats' among them, asking for more serious consideration of the Russian proposal, but it was not a popular position. As the elections of 1953 and 1957 showed, Adenauer's suspicious approach to the Soviet Union was supported by a majority of West Germans, and perhaps also by East Germans, even if it meant the death of reunification.

The fate of Stalin's proposal was not decided in Germany. In the final analysis it was up to the Allies. The West, under the leadership of the United States, might perhaps have agreed to the reunification of Germany, but neutralization, Stalin's primary objective, was completely out of the question. And, as it turned out, for good reason.

The neutralization of Germany would have meant that France would be the only NATO base on the continent. That would have been unacceptable even if France under de Gaulle had not pulled its military organization out of NATO. In the long run the neutralization of Germany might have compelled America to pull out of Europe, and that in turn would have resulted in Soviet hegemony over the entire continent.

In retrospect it must be admitted, even by people like myself who at the time did not agree, that Dulles and Adenauer were right to reject Stalin's offer. But regardless of the reasons, good or bad, the fact remains that Stalin's proposal, politically advantageous to Moscow and therefore presumably serious, was rejected. And the Soviets did not insist on its adoption. They were obviously ready to put the final stamp on the division of 1949 by integrating the GDR as firmly into their system of alliances as was the West in 1955 with regard to the Federal Republic.

This makes 1955 the second important date in the history of the end of the German Reich. The two states were founded in 1949, and in 1955 the division was cemented by their integration into opposing alliances and military organizations.

Still, the hope for reunification, involving the dissolution of the GDR and its integration into the Federal Republic, continued to live on in West Germany. The only realistic basis for that hope was the situation of Berlin, which continued as an open four-power area, and thus the one remaining channel for the continuing migration from the GDR to the Federal Republic. It was predictable that the East was not going to tolerate this leakage for much longer.

If the West really set its hope on Berlin, it should have given thought to its defense, because it was obvious that one day Berlin was going to be attacked. The to-be-expected attack came in the form of the Berlin crisis of 1958–61, and it turned out that the West had no plans for the defense of the city. Moreover, in those years the Soviet Union gained nuclear parity with the West, a factor that ever since has colored the relationship of the two big powers and their respective blocs. Prior to that time the United States had enjoyed clear superiority in the field of nuclear arms. Now the threat of mutual annihilation limited the options of both the powers. Neither could afford to start a war. This is the background against which the contest over Berlin was carried out, a power play which in 1961 ended in the erection of the Berlin Wall and the closing off of Berlin as an escape route.

That makes 1961 the third significant date in the history of the German Reich. The last hope that the two states would ultimately unite in a Western state was shattered. After 1961 it became clear that the two states were here to stay, that the great powers no longer seriously thought of breaking them up. What used to be called reunification no longer was in the cards. Any future effort to improve the German situation had to concentrate on the relationship between the now firmly established new German states. It took ten years for the Federal Republic to see this, and even when it did, the new *Ostpolitik*, like the Weimar Republic before it, stood on only one leg for another ten years. It was supported only by the Socialist-Liberal coalition that had come to power in 1969. The Christian Democratic opposition, which had voted against the ratification of the Eastern agreements in 1972, did not change its position and accept the Eastern policy of their predecessors until their victory in 1982, when they again took over the government.

Germany's new Eastern policy was spelled out in the Moscow and Warsaw treaties of 1970, and most importantly in the so-called Basic Agreement of 1972 between the Federal Republic and the GDR, which recognized their respective sovereignty without mention of what the Preamble to the Basic Law called the "national question."

These agreements of the Brandt government were in line with another very important agreement concluded in September 1971 by the four powers, in which the only remaining German issue still exclusively their domain—the status of Berlin—was settled in a painstakingly formulated and calculatedly ambiguous pragmatic document.

The importance of the Berlin agreement for Germany lies in the fact that the four powers with jurisdiction over Berlin accommodated the city's situation to the acknowledged permanent two-state structure of Germany. That required exceptional delicacy. In the eyes of East Germany, East Berlin is the unofficial capital of the GDR and West Berlin a special exclave of the Federal Republic. In the Soviet view, West Berlin enjoys a special legal status under the jurisdiction of the three Western powers, and in the view of the three Western powers all of Berlin remains a special region under four-power jurisdiction. None of the four powers, including the West, considers West Berlin a part of the Federal Republic. All four, including the Soviet Union, have affirmed their agreement not only by the continued existence of West Berlin, but also by its ties to the German Federal Republic. Politically, the Berlin agreement means that the Soviet Union and the Western powers promise to refrain from making their respective juridical positions the subject of a power contest. That doubtlessly makes life in the divided city easier. One might say that the four-power Reich created by World War II, which existed for three years, has been reduced to a portion of Berlin. The Berlin agreement of 1971 has sealed off and sterilized that portion, so that in the future it cannot become the launching pad for all-German entanglements or all-German conflicts. So much for the position of the four powers.

The relationship of the two German states also underwent a change in the beginning of the seventies. With the Basic Agreement of 1972 the Federal Republic reversed its position on the non-recognition of the GDR and its claim to being the sole representative of Germany, and with some reservations declared its readiness to treat the GDR as a separate state. A year later both states were admitted into the United Nations. This should not be dismissed as a mere gesture. It means that both states are treated as legitimate members of the community of nations like any other sovereign state.

The last significant development in this chain of events was the Helsinki Conference, which dragged on from 1971 to 1975. All European nations, including the Soviet Union, as well as the United States and Canada—in other words all NATO and all Warsaw Pact countries as well as all neutral European countries—participated in this biggest of international postwar conferences. In Helsinki something like a European peace order, akin to the final act in Vienna in 1816, was drafted and adopted.

The first part of the final act of Helsinki, and for our topic the most important one, recognizes all thirty-five participants as equal, sovereign nations, each of whom pledges to refrain from interfering in the domestic affairs of the other signatories. This established a generally accepted political norm for a peaceful Europe, and it encompassed the Federal Republic and the GDR. The final draft of the Helsinki agreement makes no mention of a possible resurrection of the German Reich or of the reunification of the German states, thereby finally ending the thirty-year-long death agony of the German Reich.

Nothing changed after 1975. Contacts between the two German states are not concerned with reunification but with the continued improvement and normalization of inter-German relations.

What are the prospects that the existing situation will change in the foreseeable future? Does the present situation justify the assumption that something like the 1952 Russian proposal for reunification and neutralization could be revived? The prospects for such a turn of events are very dim.

In 1952, the relations between the two superpowers were still in a state of flux. It was not

yet clear whether the wartime spirit of cooperation could be revived, or whether the confrontations of the postwar years would continue. We
have since learned that to a lesser or greater degree
these confrontations have become a permanent
state of affairs and will remain so as long as nuclear
parity rules out the settlement of this conflict by
war. For neither superpower can risk a war that
threatens mutual destruction. This limits their
freedom of action, particularly in areas where
since 1975 everything has been staked out and
defined—in Europe, and thus in Germany. Every
step backward by one of the great powers would
mean a step forward by the other. Therefore neither one can afford to budge.

Something else also changed since 1952. At
that time the Soviet Union and its Warsaw Pact
partners could still afford to do without the GDR;
it was nothing but a maneuverable diplomatic
commodity, a pawn. If the United States had withdrawn from continental Europe—a distinct possibility—the Soviet sphere of influence would
probably have expanded even without the GDR.
But now the GDR, in view of the striving for independence within the Eastern bloc, particularly
in Poland, has become indispensable to the Soviet
Union. Of course this relationship is doubly important for the GDR. For the German Democratic
Republic the Soviet mutual defense pact has always been indispensable.

There are similarities to this in the relationship between the United States and the Federal Republic. In 1952 a reduced NATO, in which the Americans would have retained only a small European bridgehead in France, was perhaps still possible. But after France's withdrawal from the military organization of NATO and its attempts to reestablish itself as an independent big power, the loss of the Federal Republic would have meant the end of NATO, at least as far as continental Europe is concerned. Therefore the Federal Republic has become indispensable to the United States, and conversely, the United States has become indispensable to the Federal Republic. Without the protective agreement with the United States, the Federal Republic, which has no nuclear weapons, would be helplessly exposed to the pressures and power plays of the East bloc and its nuclear weapons.

In other words, today the relationship between the two German states and their respective founders is much closer and more secure than at the time of their establishment. To break away from these mutual commitments, even if either of them wanted to, is hardly possible today.

Some circles in the Federal Republic still labor under the illusion that if the Soviets tendered a proposal like that of 1952 the response now would be entirely different, that the West would gladly accept it. Certainly not. Perhaps the Germans would now be more amenable to neutrality, because today a united Germany would again wield considerable economic power. But for that very reason the two major powers and their allies are not likely to accept it. Moreover, reunification is no longer a viable option for the two German states themselves, not because feelings have changed but for concrete political reasons.

The interrelation of the two German states and the two big alliance systems—and they are far more significant than the European alliances of the Bismarck era, not only because they are militarily powerful but also because they represent something akin to big empires—has grown closer over the years, and therefore the prospect of the resurrection or new formation of an all-German state, of a new German Reich of any sort, has dwindled.

Let us look at the situation from yet another vantage point, namely that of Europe. It has been said that the division of Germany coincided with the division of Europe, that national movements of independence are cropping up all over Europe— East and West—and that in the long run the Europeanization of Europe could lead to German reunification.

However, if we were to ask how the European neighbors of the two German states feel about the reunification desired by many Germans, the unequivocal answer would have to be that no European country, East or West, wants or would readily accept such a reunification.

All European countries have had bad and often terrible experiences with the former German

Reich. Particularly in the two most important neighboring countries, France and Poland, alarm bells would go off if a new eighty-million-strong power bloc were to rise up again at their borders. In 1984 Italy's Foreign Minister Andreotti, a good friend of the Federal Republic, succinctly summed up the feeling of all Germany's neighbors: "They are two, and two they must remain."

Finally, what would a reunification of the two German states as they have evolved over forty years look like? It is something that is difficult to visualize. It is perhaps possible to imagine a reunification in which one of the states would disappear and be absorbed by the other. Of course, that presupposes a war, and today such a reunification could probably take place only in a mass grave. But it is impossible to imagine a reunification in which the two German states as they are today amalgamate.

The history of the last forty-odd years has led further and further away from the German Reich. From its still shadowy existence as the object of the four victors in 1945, it has gradually moved toward complete nonexistence, toward nonrestorability. Looking back on its history we must ask ourselves whether or not that is to be regretted. That history, with all its achievements and failures, with all its violations and horrors, is in fact only twice as long as the time that separates us from it today. And that span lengthens with each passing year.

Postscript 1990

This book was first published in Germany in 1987, and the developments of 1990 seem to stand in contradiction to its conclusions. I had not foreseen these developments, let alone expected them, nor do I know a single person who would have either predicted or expected them. After all, the same Federal Chancellor who in 1990 engineered the incorporation of the GDR into the Federal Republic had, back in 1987, received the GDR's Chairman of the Council of State with all the honors typically accorded to the head of a sovereign state.

True, today we can no longer look at the German Reich as through a telescope, as I did in 1987. Rather, we have to ask ourselves whether the Reich has resurfaced, even though under a different name. This should serve as a drastic warning that the prediction of historical developments, even in the short run, or perhaps particularly in the short run, is a risky undertaking.

Yet I nonetheless dare to offer up my book without revisions. I do so for two reasons. To begin with, the unexpected reconstitution of the 80 million German colossus, if successful, offers the opportunity to review and carefully reexamine its brief history—the history of its transformation from Bismarck to Hitler. That history remains unchanged, and the lesson it teaches, that Germany very quickly might reveal to the world an entirely different face, is more to the point than ever. Secondly, history, even in 1990, remains unpredictable—also and particularly in the short run. The German orations and headlines of October 3, 1990 spoke of German unity as being "completed" on that day. In fact, however, this new German unity is anything but complete. For the time being it is merely a formal amalgamation of a wealthy state and another, poor one which in 1990 was catapulted into mass unemployment. The GDR continues to exist even if it joined the Federal Republic in 1990. However, it no longer is the modestly prosperous, more or less functioning GDR of 1987. It is an economically devastated, politically destroyed country. Whether the Federal Republic is able (and wants) to rescue its new member from the ruin inflicted on it in the space of less than a year, or whether, by doing so, will overextend itself and possibly itself be pulled down, remains an open question, at least as open as what Bonn used to refer to as the "German question" prior to 1990. And it might even, at least in the short run, turn into the new "German question."

Acknowledgments

Age and illness are to blame for my failure to complete this book, the fruit of years of study and decades of observation, in an orderly fashion. My friend Professor Arnulf Baring came to my assistance. In eleven sessions he and Volker Zastrow, his invaluable assistant, went over and discussed with me the eleven lectures that form the basis of this book. Volker Zastrow has devoted an enormous amount of time to the transcripts prepared by Gunda Ernst. Without altering any of my ideas, he eliminated the repetitions, infelicities, and solipsisms that inevitably creep into an unedited conversation, and it was he who prepared the first readable text. I reworked, expanded, and emended that text. The result is this volume. Still, I fear that it bears the mark of having been spoken rather than written.

Acknowledgments are a routine part of every work of history. The thanks I owe Arnulf Baring and Volker Zastrow are of an entirely different order. Without their "midwifery" (Baring's phrase), this book would not have come into being. Yet for better or for worse it is my book. Neither of my birth assistants should be held responsible for anything said or—often intentionally— left unsaid. And all errors, shortcomings, and deficiencies are mine alone.

Berlin, August 1987

Index

261

German National movement
and, 15–16, 18–25, 28
hegemony of, 3, 8, 107
Russia and, 57–58
wars of, 26–33
in Weimar Republic, 173, 174

Rapallo Treaty, 144
Red Army, 143
Reichenau, Walther von, 188
Reich Labor Service, 193
Reichstag:
in Bismarck era, 43, 45, 46,
57
fire in, 183, 205
under Hitler, 184, 193
in Imperial era, 66
and 1918 revolution, 126, 135
of Weimar Republic, 159,
163, 166–68, 172–74, 176
during World War I, 101–6,
118–19, 158
Reichswehr, 142–44, 161, 176,
177, 226
Hitler and, 188–91, 196–97,
202–4
See also Wehrmacht
Reinsurance Treaty, 63, 73
Reparations, 138, 140, 141, 145,
146, 148, 150, 152, 153,
155, 168, 172
Reunification, 243, 245, 251,
254
Ribbentrop, Joachim von, 219
Right Opposition, 103
Röhm, Ernst, 191
Roon, Albrecht von, 45
Roosevelt, Franklin D., 16, 98,
129, 229–31
Rosenberg, Arthur, 39
Ruhr, 146, 147, 163
Rupprecht, Crown Prince, 175
Russia, 3, 5, 7, 63, 68
and Berlin Agreement, 249
Bismarck and, 48, 49, 56–62
and German Confederation,
20
at Helsinki Conference, 250
and Imperial Germany, 72,
73, 75–82, 84, 85
1905 revolution in, 67, 79

1918 revolution in, 97, 99–
101, 104
postwar, 242, 245–46, 251–
53
and treaty of Brest-Litovsk,
108–9
and Weimar Republic, 140,
142–44, 149
in World War I, 89, 90, 92,
95, 99–101, 106, 140, 228,
229
in World War II, 218, 219,
222, 224–29, 231–34, 236
Russo-Japanese War, 76
Russo-Turkish War, 55–56

SA, 187–91, 193, 195–97, 214
Schacht, Hjalmar, 202
Scheidemann, Philip, 126, 135
Schleicher, Gen. Kurt von,
154–55, 165–67, 172–77,
185, 188, 192
Schlieffen, Alfred von, 76, 94–
95
Schlieffen Plan, 90–95, 108
Schmalkaldic War, 3
Schumpeter, Joseph, 64
Schwarzenberg, Prince, 23
Seeckt, Gen. Hans von, 142,
161, 226
Serbia, 78–79
in World War I, 89, 90, 95
Seven Years' War, 3, 12
Skaggerak, battle of, 97
Social Democrats, 40–44, 63–
67, 81
National Socialists and, 184,
200, 206
and 1918 revolution, 126, 135
postwar, 241, 245, 248
in Weimar Republic, 158–60,
163, 164, 172
World War I and, 88, 89, 101–
3, 120–21, 131
Soviet Union, *see* Russia
Speer, Albert, 236
SS, 193, 196–98, 213
Stalin, Josef, 225, 228, 245, 246
Stauffenberg, Count Klaus von,
209
Stein, Baron vom, 15
Stinnes-Legien Agreement, 161

265

266